ON THE
JOB
SERIES

REAL PEOPLE
WORKING in

EDUCATION

ON THE JOB SERIES

REAL PEOPLE WORKING *in*

EDUCATION

Blythe Camenson

Printed on recyclable paper

VGM Career Horizons
a division of *NTC Publishing Group*
Lincolnwood, Illinois USA

Library of Congress Cataloging-in-Publication Data
Camenson, Blythe.
    Real people working in education / Blythe Camenson.
        p.   cm. — (On the job)
    Includes bibliographical references (p.) and index.
    ISBN 0-8442-4734-0 (h : alk. paper). — ISBN 0-8442-4735-9 (p :
alk. paper)
    1. Teaching—Vocational guidance—United States.   2. College
teaching—Vocational guidance—United States.   3. Journalism—
Vocational guidance—United States.   4. Archives—Vocational
guidance—United States.   5. Museum techniques—Vocational guidance—
United States.   6. Librarianship—Vocational guidance—United
States.   I. Title.   II. Series: On the job (Lincolnwood, Ill.)
LB1775.2.C36   1997
371.1 — dc21   96-45455
                                                                            CIP

Published by VGM Career Horizons, a division of NTC Publishing Group
4255 West Touhy Avenue, Lincolnwood (Chicago), Illinois 60646-1975, U.S.A.
© 1997 by NTC Publishing Group. All rights reserved.
No part of this book may be reproduced, stored in a retrieval
system, or transmitted in any form or by any means,
electronic, mechanical, photocopying, or otherwise,
without the prior permission of NTC Publishing Group.
Manufactured in the United States of America.

7 8 9 0 VL 9 8 7 6 5 4 3 2 1

Dedication

To my editor, Betsy Lancefield, who has allowed me to increase my knowledge and share it with the reading public.

Contents

6. Radio and Television Reporters and Broadcasters   71

7. Museum Workers   83

Acknowledgments

The author would like to thank the following professionals for providing information about their careers:

Carol Behan, high school teacher

Claire Best, ESL instructor

Judy Burns, college instructor/online instructor

Marshall J. Cook, college professor

John Fleckner, archivist

Jeremy Fried, character interpreter

Jan Goldberg, author/freelance writer

Noreen Grice, education coordinator/astronomer

Mark Hulme, elementary school teacher/online campus coordinator

Carol Jones, librarian

Michael Malone, photojournalist

Charles McGovern, curator

Stephen Morrill, online instructor

Steve Oserman, librarian

Terrence Place, high school guidance counselor

Lee Rodgers, radio talk show host

Al Sunshine, television reporter

Carolyn Travers, director of research

Joyce Williams, director of special projects

Jill Winland-Brown, associate professor

Maureen Wright, elementary school teacher

How to Use This Book

On the Job: Real People Working in Education is part of a series of career books designed to help you find essential information quickly and easily. Unlike other career resources on the market, books in the *On the Job* series provide you with information on hundreds of careers, *in an easy-to-use format*. This includes information on:

- The nature of the work
- Working conditions
- Employment
- Training, other qualifications, and advancement
- Job outlooks
- Earnings
- Related occupations
- Sources of additional information

But that's not all. You'll also benefit from a first-hand look at what the jobs are really like, as told in the words of the employees themselves. Throughout the book, one-on-one interviews with dozens of practicing professionals enrich the text and enhance your understanding of life on the job.

These interviews tell what each job entails, what the duties are, what the lifestyle is like, what the upsides and downsides are. All of the professionals reveal what drew them to the field and how they got started. And, to help you make the best career choice for yourself, each professional offers you some expert advice based on years of experience.

Each chapter also lets you see at a glance, with easy-to-reference symbols, the level of education required and salary range for the featured occupations.

So, how do you use this book? Easy. You don't need to run to the library and bury yourself in cumbersome documents from the Bureau of Labor Statistics, nor do you need to rush out and buy a lot of bulky books you'll never plow through. All you have to do is glance through our extensive table of contents, find the fields that interest you, and read what the experts have to say.

Introduction to the Field

People who share knowledge give of themselves in many different capacities, providing a valuable service. The service industry as a whole leads all others as the largest employer in the United States. If you're reading this book, chances are you're already considering a career in one of the many areas of this wide-open occupational category. Glancing through the table of contents will give you an idea of all the choices open to you.

But perhaps you're not sure of the working conditions the different fields offer or which area would suit your personality, skills, and lifestyle the most. There are several factors to consider when deciding which sector to pursue. Each field carries with it different levels of responsibility and commitment. To identify occupations that will match your expectations, you need to know what each job entails.

Ask yourself the following questions and make note of your answers. Then, as you go through the following chapters, compare your requirements to the information provided by the professionals interviewed inside. Their comments will help you pinpoint the fields that would interest you, and eliminate those that would clearly be the wrong choice.

- How much of a people person are you? Do you prefer to work alone or face to face with students or patrons? Or would you be more content with telephone or online computer contact?

- Do you want to work in an office, or would you prefer to be in a classroom setting or on the grounds of a living history museum or inside a library?

- How much time are you willing to commit to training? Some skills can be learned on-the-job or in a year or two of formal training; others can take considerably longer.

- How much money do you expect to earn starting out and after you have a few years' experience under your belt? Salaries and earnings vary greatly in each chosen profession.

- How much independence do you require? Do you want to be your own boss or will you be content as a salaried employee?

- Would you rather work daytime hours or would you prefer evenings or weekends?

Knowing what your expectations are, then comparing them to the realities of the work will help you make informed choices.

Although *On the Job: Real People Working in Education* strives to be as comprehensive as possible, not all jobs in this extensive field have been covered here or given the same amount of emphasis. Several categories of service professions have merited their own book. You will find information on other service professions in *Real People Working in Health Care*, *Real People Working in the Law*, and *Real People Working in Service Businesses*.

If you still have questions after reading this book, there are a number of other avenues to pursue. You can find out more information by contacting the sources listed at the end of each chapter. You can also find professionals on your own to talk to and observe as they go about their work. Any remaining gaps you discover can be filled by referring to the *Occupational Outlook Handbook*.

CHAPTER 1

Kindergarten and Elementary School Teaching

🎓 **EDUCATION**
BA/BS Required
Other (Certification)

💲💲💲 **SALARY/EARNINGS**
$30,000 to $40,000

OVERVIEW

Kindergarten and elementary school teachers play a vital role in the development of children. What children learn and experience during their early years can shape their views of themselves and the world, and affect later success or failure in school, work, and their personal lives.

Kindergarten and elementary school teachers introduce children to numbers, language, science, and social studies. They may use games, music, artwork, films, slides, computers, and other instructional technology to teach basic skills.

Most elementary school teachers instruct one class of children in several subjects. In some schools, two or more teachers teach as a team and are jointly responsible for a group of students in at least one subject. In other schools, a teacher may teach one special subject—usually music, art, reading, science, arithmetic, or physical education—to a number of classes. A small but growing number of teachers instruct multilevel classrooms—those with students at several different learning levels.

In addition to classroom activities, teachers plan and evaluate lessons, sometimes in collaboration with teachers of related subjects. They also prepare tests, grade papers, prepare report cards, oversee study halls and homerooms, supervise extracurricular activities, and meet with parents and school staff to discuss a student's academic progress or personal problems.

In recent years, site-based management, which allows teachers and parents to participate actively in management decisions, has gained popularity. In many schools, teachers help make decisions regarding the budget, personnel, textbook choices, curriculum design, and teaching methods.

Including school duties performed outside the classroom, many teachers work more than 40 hours a week. Most teachers work the traditional 10-month school year with a 2-month vacation during the summer. Teachers on the 10-month schedule may teach in summer sessions, take other jobs, travel, or pursue other personal interests. Many enroll in college courses or workshops in order to continue their education. Teachers in districts with a year-round schedule typically work 8 weeks, are on vacation for 1 week, and have a 5-week midwinter break.

Most states have tenure laws that prevent teachers from being fired without just cause and due process. Teachers may obtain tenure after they have satisfactorily completed a probationary period of teaching, normally 3 years. Tenure is not a guarantee of a job, but it does provide some security.

Teachers held about 3,255,000 jobs in 1992; more than 9 out of 10 were in public schools. Employment was distributed as follows:

Elementary	1,634,000
Secondary	1,263,000
Special education	358,000

Special Education

Special education teachers, who are found in lower grades and high schools, instruct students with a variety of disabilities, such as visual and hearing impairments, learning disabilities, and physical disabilities. Special education teachers design and modify instruction to meet a student's special needs. Teachers also work with students who have other special instructional needs, such as those who are very bright or gifted or those who have limited English proficiency.

TRAINING

All 50 states and the District of Columbia require public school teachers to be certified. Certification is generally for one or several related subjects. Usually certification is granted by the state board of education or a certification advisory committee. Teachers may be certified to teach the early childhood grades (usually nursery school through grade 3); the elementary grades (grades 1 through 6 or 8); or a special subject, such as reading or music. In most states, special education teachers receive a credential to teach kindergarten through grade 12. These teachers train in the specialty that they want, such as teaching children with learning disabilities or behavioral disorders.

Requirements for regular certificates vary by state. However, all states require a bachelor's degree and completion of an approved teacher training program with a prescribed number of subject and education credits and supervised practice teaching.

Traditional education programs for kindergarten and elementary school teachers include courses designed specifically for those preparing to teach in mathematics, physical science, social science, music, art, and literature, as well as prescribed professional education courses, such as philosophy of education, psychology of learning, and teaching methods.

JOB OUTLOOK

Overall employment of kindergarten and elementary school teachers is expected to increase faster than the average for all occupations through the year 2005, fueled by dramatic growth among special education teachers. However, projected employment growth varies among individual teaching occupations. Job openings for all teachers are expected to increase substantially by the end of the decade as the large number of teachers now in their forties and fifties reach retirement age.

Employment of special education teachers is expected to increase much faster than the average for all occupations through the year 2005 due to legislation emphasizing training and employment for individuals with disabilities; technological advances resulting in more survivors of accidents and illnesses; and growing public interest in individuals with special needs. Qualified persons should have little trouble finding a job, due to increased demand for these workers combined with relatively high turnover among special education teachers. Many special education teachers switch to general education teaching or change careers altogether, often because of job stress associated with teaching special education, particularly excessive paperwork and inadequate administrative support.

SALARIES

According to the National Education Association, public elementary school teachers averaged $34,800 in 1992–93. Earnings in private schools generally are lower.

Many public school teachers belong to unions, such as the American Federation of Teachers and the National Education Association, that bargain with school systems over wages, hours, and the terms and conditions of employment.

RELATED FIELDS

Kindergarten and school teaching requires a wide variety of skills and aptitudes, including a talent for working with children; organizational, administrative, and record-keeping abilities; research and communication skills; the power to influence, motivate, and train others; patience; and creativity. Workers in other occupations requiring some of these aptitudes include college and university faculty, counselors, education administrators, employment interviewers, librarians, preschool workers, public relations specialists, sales representatives, social workers, and trainers and employee development specialists.

Special education teachers work with students with disabilities and special needs. Other occupations that help people with disabilities include school psychologists, speech pathologists, and occupational, physical, and recreational therapists.

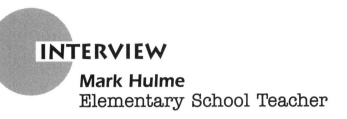

INTERVIEW

Mark Hulme
Elementary School Teacher

Mark Hulme is the computer teacher in charge of the computer lab at Hodge Elementary School, a magnet school in Savannah, Georgia. He teaches pre-k through grade 5. He is also the Online Campus coordinator for America Online.

What the Job's Really Like

"They come to the computer lab once a week for an hour. I can teach them whatever I feel like doing on any particular day. This is considered an enrichment course or an elective. I don't really teach the computer, I teach different subjects *using* the computer, social studies, or science, for example.

"I use a lot of different programs to teach different skills or disciplines. I have programs that are games that teach fractions, for example, or about matter. They could work with a drawing program where they'd color a butterfly, or there's a program with a little bunny rabbit that hops around the keys that helps them with their typing skills. There's another game with a paddle that you use to knock a hole through bricks. This helps them develop their fine motor skills and get used to using the mouse.

"They'll probably need typing skills up through high school, but by then voice recognition software will be in vogue and they won't even need to know how to type. The only problem with that, though, is if you have 30 people in a room and they're all talking to their computer, it's going to be kind of loud. All the trade publications I read say that by the year 2003, voice recognition software will be as inexpensive as using a keyboard. They say that if you teach typing skills now it won't be important later. But I don't believe that. I think people will still want the keyboard. If you're tired, it's easier to move your fingers than your mouth. And you'd lose your voice, too.

"I enjoy working with all the different levels, from the four-year-olds to the upper grades. And I enjoy watching the kids have fun with the computers. You can teach essential life skills, but through the computer it's fun for them—if it's boring it's not going to help them much.

"There are some people in the school who don't understand what I'm doing. They come in and see rabbits hopping around or bricks being blown away and they see the kids laughing and giggling and they think it's an arcade I'm running. But luckily my principal is behind me one hundred percent. I took her to a computer conference and she saw that everyone there was saying what I'd been saying for years, so she realized I was right.

"I have anywhere from 10 to 36 in a class. My official schedule is from nine to three, but I tend to go in early and leave late. I love my work. I think teaching is the most important profession."

How Mark Hulme Got Started

"I got my B.A. in English from Armstrong College in Savannah and I was planning to be a writer. At the same time I was working in a group home for the mentally retarded. My advisor suggested I take a couple of education classes as a back-up. I liked it so much I ended up doing it full time.

"I started teaching middle school, seventh and eighth grade English, and at the same time I was involved with computers at home as a hobby. I tutored for AOL, and then my hours with them grew until I was eventually offered the Online Campus coordinator job.

"I started bringing the computers to school to work with the kids. Then Savannah started a magnet school program. One was for fine arts, the other was for computers. I applied for the computer elementary school and got the job."

Expert Advice

"I'd suggest you go to a school to observe or volunteer. Spend at least a whole day and observe different levels and different types of schools. You can go to a school in an affluent area, but you should also see what it's like in an urban or low-income area.

"But if you don't love kids, you shouldn't be doing this. We get so many people wanting jobs, thinking it's good pay and good work, but it's not really for them."

• • •

INTERVIEW
Maureen Wright
Elementary School Teacher

Maureen Wright is a VH (visually handicapped) teacher at the Texas School for the Blind and Visually Impaired, a residential campus that has an elementary, junior high, and senior high school. The children she works with range in age from 7 to 12.

What the Job's Really Like

"My job is very different from being in a standard elementary school. We focus on what the students' individual needs are as they relate to their visual impairment. Children come to us to catch up on their braille reading and writing skills and to catch up on the new computer technology that helps blind and visually impaired kids stay in their school district and eventually go to college. I teach anything that is going to help them keep up to grade level, and then we send them back to their school district.

"The average stay is three to four years, although we have many kids who stay with us throughout their entire school career. They live at our school while they're here. A lot of them come to us around the second grade and, if they get caught up, they usually go back to their regular school district around the fifth grade. Sometimes they come back to us again for a short time in high school when the academics really pick up and they need some further assistance.

"With the children who are on grade level we follow the state curriculum. But most of our kids have fallen behind and aren't on grade level. We do whatever it takes to catch them up to where they need to be. We follow an applied curriculum. That means we go through the state curriculum and pick out the items the students need the most to move on. It takes a lot of time for them to learn braille. It takes a lot longer to learn to read in braille then it does to read in print. So we try to abbreviate what they would get normally in their regular school district.

"I have six children in a class at a time and I work with a teacher's aide. Though it seems like a good ratio, within my class of six children, my kids are functioning on three different reading levels, four different math levels, that sort of thing. So it's not like a group and you say, 'class sit down and open up to page number. . . .' They all have their own books, their own special needs.

"It's very challenging. I like finding ways for the children to fit into regular society. A lot of the children grow up being held so separate from other people. They're the blind ones. And they come to us feeling that way, that they're so different. But at our school they're not. Yes, we realize you're blind, but so is everyone else and we're going to do it anyway.

"We're considered an actual school district and because of that we're expected to follow all the standard policies—the report cards and all the other administrative work. And then because we're special education, we have another whole set of policies to follow, so the politics and the paperwork are what I enjoy the least."

How Maureen Wright Got Started

"I started a little different from most. My grandfather is blind and he taught me to read and write braille when I was only ten years old. I was always driven toward this work; I just sort of grew into the job naturally.

"I have a B.A. in special education with an additional certification in teaching the blind and visually impaired from D'youville College in Buffalo, New York.

"I started at the Texas School in 1988. I also taught in Manor, Texas before that at the State School. Back in the mid-1980s handicapped children were in the state hospital schools and then the law required Texas to get the children out of the state hospitals into the regular school districts. My job was to teach them to be socially appropriate enough so they'd be able to function in the regular schools."

Expert Advice

"My suggestion would be to go and volunteer at one of the schools before you begin your studies. I don't think most people realize what's involved. We get student teachers who come work with us for three or four weeks. It's their first experience at the school and then they realize that, boy, this isn't what they want to do at all. Schools like ours all over the country are begging for volunteers. It would only take one phone call to set something up.

"And of course, the obvious, you have to love kids. But one thing I've noticed is that many people come in to volunteer who are so tender-hearted, so sweet. They have so many feelings for these poor, blind children. But they don't realize that the kind of people we need in this work are those who can look at the children and see them as just any other kids. If they do something wrong, you have to tell them 'no, it's wrong.' Just because they're blind, they can't get away with things.

"And helping them too much in some cases is the worst possible thing you could do. You need to let them find their own way, you need to let them fall or fail or bump into walls once in a while. This is all under very careful supervision, of course, but the children need to understand that hands don't come out of midair to save them all the time. You need to be tough enough to let the children learn on their own sometimes."

● ● ●

FOR MORE INFORMATION

Information on certification requirements and approved teacher training institutions is available from local school systems and state departments of education.

Information on teachers' unions and education-related issues may be obtained from:

American Federation of Teachers
555 New Jersey Ave NW
Washington, DC 20001

National Education Association
1201 16th St. NW
Washington, DC 20036

A list of institutions with teacher education programs accredited by the National Council for Accreditation of Teacher Education can be obtained from:

National Council for Accreditation of Teacher Education
2010 Massachusetts Ave. NW, 2nd Floor
Washington, DC 20036

For information on voluntary teacher certification requirements, contact:

National Board for Professional Teaching Standards
300 River Pl.
Detroit, MI 48207

A list of institutions offering training programs in special education may be obtained from:

Council for Exceptional Children
1920 Association Dr.
Reston, VA 22091

For additional information contact:

Association for Childhood Education International
11141 Georgia Ave., Suite 200
Wheaton, MD 20902

Council for American Private Education
One Massachusetts Ave., NW, Suite 700
Washington, DC 20001-1431

National Association for the Education of Young Children
1834 Connecticut Ave., NW
Washington, DC 20009-5786

High School Teaching and Guidance Counseling

OVERVIEW

EDUCATION
B.A./B.S. Required
Other—Certification

$$$ SALARY/EARNINGS
$30,000 to $50,000

Teachers

The role of a teacher is changing from that of a lecturer or presenter to one of a facilitator or coach. Interactive discussions and hands-on learning are replacing rote memorization. For example, rather than merely telling students about science, mathematics, or psychology, a teacher might ask students to help solve a mathematical problem or perform a laboratory experiment and discuss how these apply to the real world. Similarly, a teacher might arrange to bring 3- and 4-year-olds into the classroom to demonstrate certain concepts of child psychology.

As teachers move away from the traditional repetitive drill approaches, they are using more props or sophisticated manipulatives such as cameras, tape recorders, science apparatus, films, slides, overhead projectors, computers, telecommunication systems, and video discs to help students understand abstract concepts, solve problems, and develop critical thought processes.

Classes are becoming less structured, and students are working in groups to discuss and solve problems together. Preparing students for the future work force is the major stimulus generating the changes in education. To be prepared, students must be able to interact with others, adapt to new technology, and logically think through problems. Teachers provide the tools and environment for their students to develop these skills.

Secondary school teachers help students delve more deeply into subjects introduced in elementary school and learn more about the world and about themselves. They specialize in a specific subject, such as English, Spanish, mathematics, history, or biology, in junior high/middle school or high school. They may teach a variety of related courses—for example, American history, contemporary American problems, and world geography.

Secondary school teachers may assist a student in choosing courses, colleges, and careers. Special education teachers may help students with their transition into special vocational training programs, colleges, or a job. Teachers also participate in education conferences and workshops.

Teachers design their classroom presentations to meet student needs and abilities. They also may work with students individually. Teachers assign lessons, give tests, hear oral presentations, and maintain classroom discipline.

Teachers observe and evaluate a student's performance and potential. Teachers increasingly are using new assessment methods, such as examining a portfolio of a student's artwork or writing to measure student achievement. Teachers assess the portfolio at the end of a learning period to judge a student's overall progress. They may then provide additional assistance in areas where a student may need help.

Seeing students develop new skills and gain an appreciation of the joy of learning can be very rewarding. However, teaching may be frustrating when dealing with unmotivated and disrespectful students.

EDUCATION
Postgraduate Required

SALARY/EARNINGS
$40,000 average

Guidance Counselors

School counselors help students understand their abilities, interests, talents, and personality characteristics so that the student can develop realistic academic and career options. Counselors use interviews, counseling sessions, tests, or other tools to assist them in evaluating and advising students. They may operate career information centers and career education programs.

High school counselors advise on college majors, admission requirements, entrance exams, and financial aid, and on trade, technical school, and apprenticeship programs. They help students develop job-finding skills such as resume writing and interviewing techniques.

Counselors also help students understand and deal with their social, behavioral, and personal problems. They emphasize preventive and developmental counseling to provide students with the life skills needed to deal with problems before they occur, and to enhance personal, social, and academic growth.

Counselors also provide special services, including alcohol and drug prevention programs, and classes that teach students to handle conflicts without resorting to violence.

Counselors work with students individually, in small groups, or with entire classes. Counselors consult and work with parents, teachers, school administrators, school psychologists, school nurses, and social workers.

Most school counselors work the traditional 9- to 10-month school year with a 2- to 3-month vacation, although an increasing number are employed on 10 1/2- or 11-month contracts. They generally have the same hours as teachers.

TRAINING

Training for Teachers

Aspiring secondary school teachers either major in the subject they plan to teach while also taking education courses, or major in education and take subject courses.

Many states offer alternative teacher certification programs for people who have college training in the subject they will teach but do not have the necessary education courses required for a regular certificate. Alternative certification programs were originally designed to ease teacher shortages in certain subjects, such as mathematics and science. The programs have expanded to attract other people into teaching, including recent college graduates and midcareer changers. In some programs, individuals begin teaching immediately under provisional certification. After working under the close supervision of experienced educators for 1 or 2 years while taking education courses outside school hours, they receive regular certification if they have progressed satisfactorily.

Under other programs, college graduates who do not meet certification requirements take only those courses that they lack, and then become certified. This may take 1 or 2 semesters of full-time study.

Aspiring teachers who need certification may also enter programs that grant a master's degree in education, as well as certification. States also issue emergency certificates to individuals who do not meet all requirements for a regular certificate when schools cannot hire enough teachers with regular certificates.

Almost all states require applicants for teacher certification to be tested for competency in basic skills such as reading and writing, teaching skills, or subject-matter proficiency. Almost all require continuing education for renewal of the teacher's certificate. Some require a master's degree.

Many states have reciprocity agreements that make it easier for teachers certified in one state to become certified in another. Teachers may become board certified by successfully completing the National Board for Professional Teaching Standards certification process. This certification is voluntary, but may result in a higher salary.

In addition to being knowledgeable in their subject, the ability to communicate, inspire trust and confidence, and motivate students, as well as understand their educational and emotional needs, is essential for teachers. They also should be organized, dependable, patient, and creative.

With additional preparation and certification, teachers may move into positions as school librarians, reading specialists, curriculum specialists, or guidance counselors. Teachers may become administrators or supervisors, although the number of positions is limited. In some systems, highly qualified, experienced teachers can become senior or mentor teachers, with higher pay and additional responsibilities. They guide and assist less experienced teachers while keeping most of their teaching responsibilities.

Training for Guidance Counselors

Generally, counselors have a master's degree in elementary or secondary school counseling, counseling psychology, career counseling, or a related field.

Graduate level counselor education programs in colleges and universities usually are in departments of education or psychology.

Courses are grouped into eight core areas: human growth and development; social and cultural foundations; helping relationships; groups; lifestyle and career development; appraisal; research and evaluation; and professional orientation.

In an accredited program, 48 to 60 semester hours of graduate study, including a period of supervised clinical experience in counseling, are required for a master's degree. The Council for Accreditation of Counseling and Related Educational Programs (CACREP) accredits graduate counseling programs in counselor education, and in school and student affairs counseling.

In 1993, 39 states and the District of Columbia had some form of counselor credentialing legislation requiring licensure, certification, or registry for practice outside schools. Requirements vary from state to state. In some states, credentialing is mandatory; in others, voluntary.

Many counselors elect to be nationally certified by the National Board for Certified Counselors (NBCC), which grants the general practice credential, National Certified Counselor. In order to be certified, a counselor must hold a master's degree in counseling, have at least 2 years of professional counseling experience, and pass NBCC's National Counselor Examination. This national certification is voluntary and distinct from state certification. However, in some states those who pass the national exam are exempt from taking a state certification exam.

All states require school counselors to hold state school counseling certification; however, certification varies from state to state. Some states require public school counselors to have both counseling and teaching certificates. Depending on the state, a master's degree in counseling and 2 to 5 years of teaching experience may be required for a counseling certificate.

Persons interested in counseling should have a strong interest in helping others and the ability to inspire respect, trust, and confidence. They should be able to work independently or as part of a team.

Prospects for advancement vary by field. School counselors may move to a larger school; become directors or supervisors of counseling or pupil personnel services; or, usually with further graduate education, become counselor educators, counseling psychologists, or school administrators.

JOB OUTLOOK

Teachers

Overall employment of secondary school teachers is expected to increase faster than the average for all occupations through the year 2005, fueled by dramatic growth among special education teachers. However, projected employment growth varies among individual teaching occupations. Job openings for all teachers are expected to increase substantially by the end of the decade as the large number of teachers now in their forties and fifties reach retirement age.

Assuming relatively little change in average class size, employment growth of teachers depends on the rates of population growth and corresponding student enrollments. The population of 14- to 17-year-olds is expected to experience relatively strong growth through the year 2005, spurring demand for secondary school teachers.

The supply of teachers also is expected to increase in response to reports of improved job prospects, more teacher involvement in school policy, greater public interest in education, and higher salaries. In fact, enrollments in teacher training programs already have increased in recent years. In addition, more teachers should be available from alternative certification programs.

Some central cities and rural areas have difficulty attracting enough teachers, so job prospects should continue to be better in these areas than in suburban districts. Mathematics, science, and special education teachers remain in short supply. Concerns over a future work force that may not meet employers' needs could spur demand for teachers who specialize in basic skills instruction—reading, writing, and mathematics. With enrollments of minorities increasing, efforts to recruit minority teachers may intensify.

The number of teachers employed depends on state and local expenditures for education. Pressures from taxpayers to limit spending could result in fewer teachers than projected; pressures to spend more to improve the quality of education could mean more.

Guidance Counselors

Overall employment of counselors is expected to grow faster than the average for all occupations through the year 2005. In addition, replacement needs should increase significantly by the end of the decade as a large number of counselors reach retirement age.

Employment of school counselors is expected to grow because of increasing enrollments, particularly in secondary schools, state legislation requiring counselors in elementary schools, and the expanded responsibilities of counselors.

Counselors increasingly are becoming involved in crisis and preventive counseling, helping students deal with issues ranging from drug and alcohol abuse to death and suicide. Despite the increasing use of counselors, however, employment growth may be dampened by budgetary constraints.

SALARIES

High School Teachers

Median earnings for full-time educational and vocational counselors were about $30,000 a year in 1992. The middle 50 percent earned between $24,000 and $41,500 a year. The bottom 10 percent earned less than $17,800 a year, while the top 10 percent earned over $51,900 a year.

Guidance Counselors

The average salary of school counselors in the 1992–93 academic year was about $40,400, according to the Educational Research

Service. Some school counselors earn additional income working summers in the school system or in other jobs.

RELATED FIELDS

Secondary school teachers and guidance counselors can utilize similar skills in positions as college and university faculty members, in other areas of counseling, such as mental health or employment and careers, as education administrators, college and student personnel workers, employment interviewers, personnel workers, librarians, preschool workers, public relations specialists, sales representatives, social workers, and trainers and employee development specialists.

INTERVIEW
Carol Behan
High School English Teacher

Carol Behan has been teaching for over 30 years. She's been at Edmeston Central School in Edmeston, New York since 1982. Currently, she teaches English to ninth- and tenth-graders. The school holds 580 students, K-12, all in one building.

What the Job's Really Like

"Over the years my job has changed a lot. Because I've moved far enough along in my profession, it's become something I can do and know I'm doing well. It really takes a good five or six years to feel as if you're doing something much more than just faking it.

"We have a small school and my department has just three teachers. The three of us have a lot of input and freedom in developing our own program. I teach two grades with anywhere from 12 to 28 students in a class at a time. For the most part I get to see some growth from one year to the next.

"We're on a rotating schedule, not a traditional Monday-through-Friday schedule. It's a six-day cycle, and I have each class four hours out of the six-day cycle. There's such a variety to it, each day is different. It's a little bit like a college schedule.

"We do a literature strand, a writing strand, and public speaking. I'm allowed to decide which textbooks I'll use and over the last ten years or so I have developed the program just as I like it.

"One of the downsides of any teaching job is that you constantly run into administrators or people with authority above you who are often inept and unaware of what the students' needs are. You end up having to work around them.

"As much as I love teaching, I know it can definitely be a burn-out profession if you put a lot of your heart into it. Even in a small school, you see that the kids' attitudes are worsening—there are discipline problems, violence, etc. A student brought a shotgun into the school a couple of years ago and aimed it at a teacher he'd had a personality conflict with. These problems aren't just in urban schools. They're everywhere.

"It's sad because I love doing what I'm doing. Teaching is a performance art. I love communicating the literature. I teach a real snazzy Shakespeare unit, for example, and I watch the kids really come alive. That's what I went into teaching for."

How Carol Behan Got Started

"I have a B.A. in liberal arts with a concentration in English from SUNY Potsdam. I got my master's from SUNY Cortland. I chose to major in reading because it would give me more job options.

"When I went to college I had no intention of teaching. My mother was a teacher, a wonderful teacher, very dedicated. But I never thought when I was growing up that I could do it half as well as she, so I chose a completely different direction at first. My dad had died of cancer when I was 16 so I was on a personal mission to cure cancer and I thought I'd pursue a career as a research scientist. But that really was the wrong way to choose a career.

"Subsequently, remembering that I had been inspired by several of my high school teachers, I decided to get my teaching degree and see what I could do. I always felt that if I put my mind to something I could do it well.

"It was a bad time to find teaching jobs, back in the early 1970s, but I persevered and ended up finding one."

Expert Advice

"You have to love your subject matter and see its value in people's lives. You can't be convincing if you don't.

"Teachers are role models, we always will be. But our idealism has to be tempered somewhat with reality. Some people come in and they bruise so easily—the kids' attitudes can be really tough. A lot of it is just for show, testing us, but we have to remember that we do have a lot of influence on kids' lives.

"I think teaching is more important than it's ever been, though it's harder now than it's ever been."

• • •

INTERVIEW
Terrence Place
Guidance Counselor

Terrence Place is director of the freshman program at Douglas High School in Parkland, Florida. He started his career in 1968 in teaching and guidance counseling, then directing guidance programs at a variety of South Florida schools. He has a B.A. in English Education from Florida Southern College in Lakeland and his M.Ed. in counseling from Florida Atlantic University in Boca Raton. He came to his present job at Douglas when the school opened in 1989.

What the Job's Really Like

"I coordinate the orientation and registration of incoming eighth graders from the middle schools, which is really when I pick them up, about halfway through the eighth-grade year. As a matter of fact, I'm meeting with about 1,000 parents and students this evening to talk about next year's program, the importance of it and requirements for graduation. We'll also discuss how they shouldn't think that what they're doing is selecting classes for a single year. We want them to realize that they're on the start of a road toward a career.

"We don't like to mention college right away because we want to make sure that the kids understand that it's not just that they'll go to college. In actuality, they'll be going to work some day and that's what they have to plan for.

"We want them to think in terms of careers. For some careers they'd have to go to college, so they'll take a slightly different program, and other kids will have another program. But everyone is going to work, so that's the focus.

"We try to avoid the caste system—that the college kids are better than the kids going to work right after high school. In the past 30 years the percentage of careers requiring college has not changed one percentage point—it's sitting right there between 19 and 20 percent. But the ones that require some sort of post-secondary training, i.e., not college, have risen up to 70 percent from 30 percent. So the skilled labor force is really where all the activity is.

"Once the kids get to Douglas in the ninth grade we spend the first five weeks or so out in classrooms doing a 'let's look where we are today.' We also discuss what high school grades mean, what a high school record looks like, and what type of documents are sent to your employer or college, etc.

"Then, after they get their first set of grades, we start developing a four-year plan. We talk about where they want to be four years from today. Do you want to be college-accepted, moving toward this career, or do you want to be in the armed forces moving toward another career, or in trade or technical school toward yet a different career. The plan is to get them there.

"The plan is reevaluated each year depending on how they did the previous year and what new interests they might have developed. If we put it in stone we'd be throwing away a lot of rocks. What it does do is get the kids to start thinking.

"We tell the kids that they'll be taking seven classes, one of which has to relate to a potential career. Let's say that a kid says to me `I'm thinking about something athletic-related' or he wants to be an athletic trainer. Then we look right away at medical skills, because it's a program that deals with all those types of careers. If a kid said to me he wanted to go into accounting, we might really be looking at business management or law or business computer applications. This way every year they're doing some experimentation. Some of the kids will come in halfway through and say 'you made me take this class but I hate it.' I say great—now we know what you don't want. And that's a big part of knowing what you do want.

"About 85 percent of our students do go on to college. We start talking to them about different colleges, in state, out of state, large school, small school, do I want to play athletics, etc. What we do is encourage the kids by their junior year to have a list of ten schools they are potentially interested in. We have a county college night and 300 colleges come and the students can touch base with them then. Or during the summer when they go on a family vacation they can visit the schools then. The purpose of this is so that in their senior year they're all set to apply to five. The five would include a stretch school—that one ideal school, and then at the other end a sure thing and then the in-between one.

"I'd like to earn a lot more money, of course—and I'd like to work more human hours. I'm here from 6:30 to 4. I only get the month of July off.

"But the kids are the best part of my job. Parents—you can keep them all. Good students, bad students, students interested in school, students not interested in school—I like them all. This is my 28th year and sometimes I sit on my back porch in the morning having a cup of coffee and I think I just can't face it, I just can't do it. But once I get in to school and talk to the first kid the day goes very quickly."

How Terrence Place Got Started

"I believe personally that 50 percent of career choices are purely accidental. Even with all the guidance. I was a premed major. I got to my junior year and became unsure that that was what I really wanted to do. I was thinking about dentistry, too. But my Dad was a teacher and he suggested I take an education course.

For part of that requirement I had to spend 60 hours in a classroom. I fell in love with it.

"I taught for two years, English and social studies, and then they had a guidance position open in my school. At that point, if you already had 15 credits in guidance and counseling, you could become a counselor as long as you signed an agreement that you would finish your master's. So I went ahead with it."

Expert Advice

"I would recommend this career. Certainly education has been tremendously rewarding to me. I believe that teachers are born and not made. I have never seen someone go into a college of education who I didn't think beforehand would be a good teacher and come out a good teacher. I think you have to possess certain personal attributes, you have to be people-centered, be a great listener, and truly believe that you can make a difference. As far as I'm concerned, I'm a teacher placed in guidance. Everything I do is to teach a kid something."

● ● ●

FOR MORE INFORMATION

High School Teaching

Information on certification requirements and approved teacher training institutions is available from local school systems and state departments of education.

Information on teachers' unions and education-related issues may be obtained from:

American Federation of Teachers
555 New Jersey Ave. NW
Washington, DC 20001

National Education Association
1201 16th St. NW
Washington, DC 20036

A list of institutions with teacher education programs accredited by the National Council for Accreditation of Teacher Education can be obtained from:

National Council for Accreditation of Teacher Education
2010 Massachusetts Ave. NW, 2nd Floor
Washington, DC 20036

For information on voluntary teacher certification requirements, contact:

National Board for Professional Teaching Standards
300 River Pl.
Detroit, MI 48207

For additional information contact:

American Association of Colleges for Teacher Education
One Dupont Circle, NW, Suite 610
Washington, DC 20036

National Association of Independent Schools
75 Federal Street
Boston, MA 02110

Guidance Counseling

State departments of education can supply information on colleges and universities that offer approved guidance and counseling training for state certification and licensure requirements.

State employment service offices have information about job opportunities and entrance requirements for counselors.

For general information about counseling, as well as information on specialties such as school, college, mental health, rehabilitation, multicultural, career, marriage and family, and gerontological counseling, contact:

American Counseling Association
5999 Stevenson Ave.
Alexandria, VA 22304

For information on accredited counseling and related training programs, contact:

> Council for Accreditation of Counseling and Related
>   Educational Programs
> American Counseling Association
> 5999 Stevenson Ave.
> Alexandria, VA 22304

For information on national certification requirements and procedures for counselors, contact:

> National Board for Certified Counselors
> 3-D Terrace Way
> Greensboro, NC 27403

For general information about school counselors, contact:

> American School Counselor Association
> 5999 Stevenson Ave.
> Alexandria, VA 22304

CHAPTER **3** Adult Education

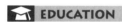
EDUCATION
Varies

$$$ SALARY/EARNINGS
$20,000 to $40,000

OVERVIEW

Adult education teachers work in a variety of settings. They are employed by public school systems; community and junior colleges; universities; businesses that provide formal education and training for their employees; automotive repair, bartending, business, computer, electronics, medical technology, and similar schools and institutes; dance studios; health clubs; job training centers; community organizations; labor unions; computer online services: and religious organizations.

Adult education teachers work in three main areas: vocational-technical education, basic education, and continuing education.

Adult Vocational-Technical Education

Some adult education teachers instruct people who have graduated or left school for occupations that do not require a college degree, such as welder, dental hygienist, automated systems manager, x-ray technician, farmer, and cosmetologist.

Other teachers provide instruction in basic education courses for school dropouts or others who need to upgrade their skills to find a job.

Increasingly, adult vocational-technical education teachers integrate academic and vocational curriculums so that students obtain a variety of skills. For example, an electronics student may be required to take courses in principles of mathematics and science in conjunction with hands-on electronics skills. Generally, teachers demonstrate techniques, have students apply them, and critique the students' work so that they can learn from their mistakes. For example, welding instructors show students various welding techniques, including the use of tools and equipment, watch students use the techniques, and have them repeat procedures until students meet specific standards required by the trade.

Adult Basic Education

Adult education teachers who instruct in adult basic education programs may work with students who do not speak English; teach adults reading, writing, and mathematics up to the 8th-grade level; or teach adults through the 12th-grade level in preparation for the General Educational Development Examination (GED). The GED offers the equivalent of a high school diploma. These teachers may refer students for counseling or job placement. Because many people who need adult basic education are reluctant to seek it, teachers also may recruit participants.

Adult Continuing Education

Some instructors help people update their job skills or adapt to technological advances. For example, an adult education teacher may train students how to use new computer software programs.

Adult education teachers also teach courses that students take for personal enrichment, such as cooking, dancing, writing, exercise and physical fitness, photography, and finance.

Many adult education teachers work part time. To accommodate students who may have job or family responsibilities, many courses are offered at night or on weekends, and range from 2- to 4-hour workshops and 1-day mini-sessions to semester-long courses.

They prepare lessons and assignments, grade papers and do related paperwork, attend faculty and professional meetings, and stay abreast of developments in their field.

Since adult education teachers work with adult students, they do not encounter some of the behavioral or social problems sometimes found when teaching younger students. The adults are there by choice, and usually are highly motivated—attributes that can make teaching these students rewarding and satisfying.

However, teachers in adult basic education deal with students at different levels of development who may lack effective study skills and self-confidence, and who may require more attention and patience than other students.

TRAINING

Training requirements vary widely by state and by subject. In general, teachers need work or other experience in their field, and a license or certificate in fields where these usually are required for full professional status.

In some cases, particularly at educational institutions, a bachelor's, master's, or doctoral degree is required, especially to teach courses that can be applied toward a 4-year degree program.

In other cases, an acceptable portfolio of work is required. For example, to secure a job teaching a flower-arranging course, an applicant would need to show examples of previous work.

Most states and the District of Columbia require adult basic education teachers to have a bachelor's degree from an approved teacher training program, and some require teacher certification.

Adult education teachers update their skills through continuing education to maintain certification. Requirements vary among institutions. Teachers may take part in seminars, conferences, or graduate courses in adult education, training and development, or human resources development, or may return to work in business or industry for a limited time.

Adult education teachers should communicate and relate well with students, enjoy working with them, and be able to motivate them. Adult basic education instructors, in particular, must be patient, understanding, and supportive to make students comfortable, develop trust, and help them better understand their needs and aims.

Some teachers advance to administrative positions in departments of education, colleges and universities, and corporate training departments. Such positions may require advanced degrees, such as a doctorate in adult and continuing education.

JOB OUTLOOK

Employment of adult education teachers is expected to grow faster than the average for all occupations through the year 2005 as the demand for adult education programs continues to rise. Participation in continuing education increases as the educational attainment of the population increases. More people are realizing that life-long learning is important to success in their careers.

To keep abreast of changes in their fields and advances in technology, an increasing number of adults are taking courses for career advancement, skills upgrading, and personal enrichment, spurring demand for adult education teachers. In addition, enrollment in adult basic education programs is increasing because of changes in immigration policy that require basic competency in English and civics, and an increased awareness of the difficulty in finding a good job without basic academic skills.

Employment growth of adult vocational-technical education teachers will result from the need to train young adults for entry-level jobs, and experienced workers who want to switch fields or whose jobs have been eliminated due to changing technology or business reorganization. In addition, increased cooperation between businesses and educational institutions to ensure that students are taught the skills employers desire should result in greater demand for adult education teachers, particularly at community and junior colleges. Since adult education programs receive state and federal funding, employment growth may be affected by government budgets.

Many job openings for adult education teachers will stem from the need to replace persons who leave the occupation. Many teach part time and move into and out of the occupation for other jobs, family responsibilities, or to retire. Opportunities will be best in fields such as computer technology, automotive mechanics, and medical technology, which offer very attractive, and often higher-paying, job opportunities outside of teaching.

SALARIES

In 1992, salaried adult education teachers who usually worked full time had median earnings around $26,900 a year. The middle 50 percent earned between $18,700 and $38,800. The lowest 10 percent earned less than $13,500, while the top 10 percent earned more than $49,200. Earnings varied widely by subject, academic credentials, experience, and region of the country.

Part-timers generally are paid hourly wages and do not receive benefits or pay for preparation time outside of class.

RELATED FIELDS

Adult education teaching requires a wide variety of skills and aptitudes, including the power to influence, motivate, and train others; organizational, administrative, and communication skills; and creativity. Workers in other occupations that require these aptitudes include other teachers, counselors, school administrators, public relations specialists, employee development specialists and interviewers, and social workers.

INTERVIEW

Marshall J. Cook
Professor, University of Wisconsin, Madison

Marshall J. Cook is a full professor in the department of Communication Programs within the Division of Continuing Studies at the University of Wisconsin, Madison. He is also a writer with hundreds of articles to his credit, a couple of dozen short stories, and numerous books including <u>Writing for the Joy of It, Freeing Your Creativity, How to Write with the Skill of a Master and the Genius of a Child, Slow Down and Get More Done, Leads and Conclusions</u>, and <u>Hometown Wisconsin.</u>

Before coming to Wisconsin, Marshall Cook was also an instructor at Solano Community College in Suisun City, California for eight years.

What the Job's Really Like

"My job is really wonderful and it's really different from the traditional campus teacher. The Division of Continuing Studies is a separate division within the university and our primary mission is adult education. I do a lot of workshops and some consulting and some on-site training of newspaper people, corporate communicators, and a variety of other people. For example, I run media workshops for police officers called 'preparing to be interviewed by the press' and one on newsletters that I've done for 16 years. Another workshop is on stress management and it follows the title of my book, *Slow Down and Get More Done.*

"Basically, I offer anything we can sell to the public. We're an income-generating unit, unlike campus teaching, and we're responsible for paying our own way.

"I develop the workshops and help publicize them and teach them, too. I'll personally teach maybe 60 to 70 of these a year along with guest speaking, and speaking at conferences and helping at other conferences.

"I teach much more than the average professor in a university, but there's no research component to my job. My research is all practical and my publications are all mass media, because that's what I teach.

"It's diverse—one of those rare opportunities to combine writing with another career that feeds the writing rather than detracting from it. The writing helps me teach and the teaching helps me write.

"It's very stimulating, but it can be enormously tiring. I do a lot of traveling, mostly within the state, bringing the workshops to where the people are. We have down times, around Christmas or in the summer, but we do have busy seasons, too and when it's hot it's hot. Sometimes I have to do three workshops in a week. I have to be careful not to overschedule myself."

How Marshall Cook Got Started

"I have a B.A. in creative writing from Stanford and an M.A. in communications/print journalism, also from Stanford. I went to law school for about four months and I was teaching one class at the University of Santa Clara in California. I realized I didn't want to be a lawyer. I liked studying the law but not the actual different jobs lawyers do, so I abandoned that.

"At about that time one of the teachers at Santa Clara died and I got his job; they hired me full time. I worked there for four years in the English department.

"It was like an old dream had been reborn. Ever since I was a kid the only two things I really wanted to do was to be a teacher and a writer. And now I've found something that lets me do both—which is really nice. I got the class at Santa Clara basically just to make some money to put myself through law school. Then I discovered I really liked it. I don't think I was really that good at it at first, but it really appealed to me.

"I came to the University of Wisconsin in 1979 as a member of the academic staff as a program coordinator. I'm probably the last person in the system who came in this way, but at that time you could move from the academic staff track to what they call a tenure track. So I moved into being an assistant professor, which is a professor without tenure. Then I put in my requisite five to six years, then applied for tenure at the associate professor level.

Once you hit that rank it's with tenure. Another three years after that I applied and then became a full professor."

Expert Advice

"These days to become a full professor on a tenure track you'd need to get your Ph.D., and it should be in a field you have some passion for.

"It's a wonderful thing to do if you get the chance to do it, because you not only deal in ideas, but you get to share them and watch them grow as you interact with young minds that aren't nearly as trained as yours, but are flexible and hungry for the knowledge you have."

● ● ●

INTERVIEW

Claire Best
ESL Instructor

Claire Best taught English as a second language to adults through an adult education program affiliated with her local school board, as well as in a private language center. She also worked overseas for many years teaching English as a foreign language to first-year university students. She is now a full-time writer.

What the Job's Really Like

"There's a big difference between teaching in the U.S. and teaching overseas. In the Adult Education program in which I worked here my classes were filled with students from a variety of countries. Overseas, of course, the students will all be from the country you're in.

"When you're in the U.S., your class is finished and you go home. Overseas, your work day might be over, but the experience of living in another country is with you every day, all day. I much prefer teaching overseas. It's far more exciting and one of the main benefits to the profession. You can work almost anywhere.

"No matter where you're teaching, though, your work is pretty much the same. You instruct students in basic English language skills: reading, writing, listening, and conversation. Like any teacher, you're responsible for designing lesson plans and for administering and grading tests. I also helped develop the teaching program and materials we used in the classroom.

"My jobs in the U.S. required many more teaching hours than my university jobs overseas. So you're on your feet a lot and you're talking a lot. I always lost my voice for a few days at the beginning of each new term.

"I found I preferred the administrative aspects more than the actual teaching. My last job overseas I was a director of a program. You have to really love classroom interaction to stay with it. A lot of TESOLers get burnt out after too many years in the classroom."

How Claire Best Got Started

"Like many TESOLers, I just fell into it. I hadn't gone the traditional route, studying ESL; I had earned a B.A. in English but had no idea what I was going to do with it. But what I did know, or thought I knew, was that I wasn't going to teach. I also got an M.Ed., but my area of study was in counseling.

"I had been working part time with the Adult Education program counseling GED students on career choices after they passed their high school equivalency, but I needed to put in more hours to make a decent living. A friend of mine was the director of the ESL evening program at one of the satellite schools and he offered to take a chance on me. My training was all on the job.

"The experience I gained through Adult Education led me to a job in a private language program, and that led me to my first job overseas."

Expert Advice

"Many people not yet in the profession think, `I can speak English, therefore I can teach it.' In some places, that's true and, often, travelers wanting to earn extra money to help pay for their trip find work tutoring or providing practice in conversation skills.

"But as the number of professionally trained teachers increases, opportunities for unqualified teachers decrease.

"These days, a bachelor's degree is considered the minimum qualification for teaching ESL/EFL. A master's degree would be necessary to teach in a university setting. State certification as a teacher is required for those teaching in American schools and some international schools.

"Teaching English as a second or foreign language is not the same as teaching it as a first language. There is a foundation of knowledge and methodology for this field of study which includes linguistics, second language acquisition, education practices, sociology, anthropology, psychology, and testing and measurement, and other related subjects.

"My advice is first to volunteer to see if this profession is right for you—and if it is, then you should plan for your career and get that specialized training. This will open up many more jobs to you.

"The best way to find a job, especially a job overseas, is to attend the annual TESOL conference. Recruiters come in from all around the world to staff their programs."

•   •   •

INTERVIEW

Stephen Morrill
AOL Online Instructor, Freelance Writing

Stephen Morrill has been with America Online's online campus program since the fall of 1994. He teaches two courses: Freelance Nonfiction Magazine Articles and Freelance Nonfiction Writing Business. He also is a full-time freelance writer and the local correspondent in his home area for Reuters, the world's largest wire service. His stories are used by some 200,000 newspaper, TV, or radio stations around the world.

What the Job's Really Like

"The first course I teach, 'Freelance Nonfiction Magazine Articles,' is intended to teach students how to write a research-based, standard nonfiction magazine article. I tell them how to do this, and guide them through a short sample article that they write, word by word.

"The other course, 'Freelance Nonfiction Writing Business,' is intended to teach how to market yourself and how to run the business of nonfiction writing on a freelance basis. Nonfiction includes magazines, books, and assorted brochures and newsletters. The course touches upon all these but focuses most heavily upon the magazine market.

"There is a two-hour weekly session for 8 weeks for both courses, during which we interact 'live' online. I upload additional material to a private library and students download that material too.

"The classes consists of three parts. Each week I upload to our private library materials they should read before the next class. In class we interact as much as the medium allows: we have questions and answers, and we do an in-class exercise or two. Each week students also receive an assignment to carry out.

"The job is really a lot of fun. I teach it for three reasons: First, I get cash for it. Second, I simply love to talk (or write) about freelancing and I'm a good teacher too, and third, it gets me pumped up for my own writing, sort of like going to weekend conferences but with pay.

"I put in a lot of hours offline, even with minimum critiquing of student manuscripts. I'm very determined to tell them all I know and to give them their money's worth. Student need a three-inch looseleaf binder to hold the material from one course.

"I keep time down by automating things as much as possible. I can critique a 1,500-word manuscript in about 20 minutes. This comes, frankly, from having seen almost every question or problem before and so having an answer ready at hand and also from just being a fast typist. And I am not ashamed to say `I don't know' sometimes. I do usually try to suggest some other place to look for the answer.

"I get paid $27.50 per student here on AOL. It's a source of money; it's not a living. It probably averages about $10 per hour of work—slightly above the minimum wage and well below the $50 per hour that I shoot for in my writing. I also earn free AOL hours from teaching that give me the freedom to play on the Internet and Web. I can use those extensively for researching my magazine and newspaper writing.

"Online teaching permits me to shove a lot of material at the students, since they can download it and read it on their own. And the question/answer sessions are almost as good as the live ones. The biggest disadvantage to online teaching is the (current) inability to show students things. I cannot just hold up a *Writer's Market* and say 'buy this book' or show them a sample of a spreadsheet printout or database printout (the spacing gets lost in the ASCII transference so only the simplest layouts work). For offline, in-person classes I can bring boxes of magazines and books with me to use for illustration. But you can't do that online."

How Stephen Morrill Got Started

"I learned about the job on AOL through another AOL teacher who knew that I taught nonfiction writing at a local school and in seminars and that I had been a full-time freelancer for ten years. He asked me to come to AOL and teach there. I first became a subscriber to the service, then sent a proposal and lesson plan to the Online Campus coordinator via e-mail. He let me try a freebie course first. Then I started teaching and getting paid."

Expert Advice

"Do it only if you already teach somewhere else or have some experience in teaching. Regard it as an adjunct to your real job; it's that other job that gives you the expertise to teach. Be extremely computer-literate and comfortable with the online, Internet, and web worlds. Take a class or two online to see what it's all about before you jump in."

• • •

INTERVIEW

Judy Burns
AOL Online Instructor, Screenwriting

Judy Burns teaches Introduction to Screenwriting on America Online.

She is a writer-producer-story consultant whose extensive prime-time

credits include "Star Trek" ("The Tholian Web"), "MacGyver," "Stingray,"

"Airwolf," "T. J. Hooker," "Magnum P.I.," and "Cagney and Lacey."

She also teaches screenwriting at UCLA Extension, Ithaca Col-

lege, University of California-Riverside, and other universities around

the country. (See her interview on college teaching in Chapter 4.)

What the Job's Really Like

"Online education can come in a couple of ways. You can teach for a university or for an online service. UCLA Extension, for instance, now offers about seven classes online. These classes are actually taught via e-mail because UCLA doesn't have an Internet server that allows for IRC, Internet Relay Chat—a virtual classroom people can actually use online.

"Basically the university courses are more like correspondence courses but they pay the instructors very well. Maybe $1,200 or $1,300 for ten weeks for 15 students. Through AOL you get maybe $15 to $30 per student.

"The course I teach on AOL is divided into three parts. Part one consists of learning how to create or find a story, pitching the idea, the story spine, introducing and developing new characters, using mythological archetypes, and writing a story outline.

"Part two looks more closely at story structure, character motivation, sub-plots, set-ups and pay-offs, development of tension and conflict, and writing the beat outline—the blueprint for a feature film screenplay.

"Part three consists of formatting the script, writing professional dialogue and narrative, scene and sequence construction, getting your script into a marketable form, and presenting it to agents and the industry.

"It's very energizing teaching online. You have the same dynamics in an online classroom that you would have in a standard classroom, except that it might be a little more controlled. You can look them in the eye offline, and offline they also have a tendency to bounce around in the class a bit. Online you don't know if they're bouncing around. What you do know, is that if you're getting their attention and getting them interested, they will start to really chatter at you. I stop my lecturing and ask them to count off and let me know what they're thinking and they respond resoundingly.

"The only disadvantage is that they have to go look at the films outside the classroom. Normally I would show a film in a standard class and talk about it at the same time we watch it.

"There's another thing I've found that's a little different. In a standard classroom I can tell everybody that what we say in the classroom stays here. For everyone's protection we have to agree not to steal someone else's idea. I tell them, if you're not comfortable with that, then please go away. What I found online is there was reticence to put their material out until we had been online together for about 10 or 15 weeks. By the tenth week, they know each other and begin to post their material to each other. It takes longer to build up trust—you can't see people's eyes."

How Judy Burns Got Started

"It was something I was interested in. I knew they must be teaching classes online so I went online and found the little university at AOL. I knew that there were actual universities running online classes, so I figured AOL would be too.

"I was looking for the experience of teaching online. I investigated it myself. I'm computer literate and knew it was out there. My co-teacher, Ron Wilkerson, and I made a proposal and the coordinator accepted it.

"I started in August, 1995, offering a free class. New instructors on AOL have to give a freebie class first so the coordinator can make sure they're comfortable with the environment."

Expert Advice

"It's easier if you design your course so you're teaching in lecture mode rather than in workshop mode. With a workshop you spend more time dealing with students' work, and unless it's a very lucrative teaching position, at a university, for example, where they charge regular university tuition fees, it's not cost-effective.

"If you want to teach online, go to the World Wide Web, call up a search engine for educational institutions, and then look to see if they are carrying courses online. If so, you could then send an e-mail to the web master in charge of the program with your resume and a proposal to teach online.

"You'd get a straight salary rather than something based on per student. In terms of services, AOL is the best—there's not much in the way of classes on the other services. But another way is to do it yourself, by setting up a home page.

"You would need a small working knowledge of how computers function. For example, you have to know the speed of your modem and the fact that info gets transferred faster the larger the number. If you have a slow modem it takes longer and will ultimately cost you more."

• • •

FOR MORE INFORMATION

Information on adult basic education programs and teacher certification requirements is available from state departments of education and local school districts.

For information about adult vocational-technical education teaching positions, contact state departments of vocational-technical education.

For information on adult continuing education teaching positions, contact departments of local government, state adult education departments, schools, colleges and universities, religious organizations, and a wide range of businesses that provide formal training for their employees.

General information on adult education is available from:

American Association for Adult and Continuing Education
1101 Connecticut Ave. NW, Suite 700
Washington, DC 20036

American Vocational Association
1410 King St.
Alexandria, VA 22314

ERIC Clearinghouse on Adult, Career, and Vocational
    Education
1900 Kenny Rd.
Columbus, OH 43210-1090

Information on teaching English as a second language and on
jobs is available from:

(TESOL) Teachers of English to Speakers of Other
    Languages, Inc.
1600 Cameron Street, Suite 300
Alexandria, VA 22314-2705

CHAPTER 4 Four-Year College and University Teaching

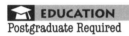
EDUCATION
Postgraduate Required

$$$ SALARY/EARNINGS
$20,000 to $60,000

OVERVIEW

College and university faculty teach and advise over 14 million full-time and part-time college students and perform a significant part of our nation's research. They also study and meet with colleagues to keep up with developments in their field and consult with government, business, nonprofit, and community organizations.

Faculty generally are organized into departments or divisions, based on subject or field. They usually teach several different courses in their department: algebra, calculus, and differential equations, for example. They may instruct undergraduate or graduate students, or both.

College and university faculty may give lectures to several hundred students in large halls, lead small seminars, and supervise students in laboratories. They also prepare lectures, exercises, and laboratory experiments, grade exams and papers, and advise and work with students individually. In universities, they also counsel, advise, teach, and supervise graduate student research. They may use closed-circuit and cable television, computers, videotapes, and other teaching aids.

Faculty keep abreast of developments in their field by reading current literature, talking with colleagues, and participating in professional conferences. Some also do their own research to expand knowledge in their field. They experiment, collect and analyze data, and examine original documents, literature, and other source material. From this, they develop hypotheses, arrive at conclusions, and write about their findings in scholarly journals and books.

Most faculty members serve on academic or administrative committees that deal with the policies of their institution, departmental matters, academic issues, curricula, budgets, equipment purchases, and hiring. Some work with student organizations.

Department heads generally have heavier administrative responsibilities.

The amount of time spent on each of these activities varies by individual circumstance and type of institution. Faculty members at universities generally spend a significant part of their time doing research; those in four-year colleges, somewhat less; and those in two-year colleges, relatively little. However, the teaching load usually is heavier in two-year colleges. (See Chapter 3 for more information on working in a two-year college.)

College faculty generally have flexible schedules. They must be present for classes, usually 12 to 16 hours a week, and for faculty and committee meetings. Most establish regular office hours for student consultations, usually 3 to 6 hours per week. Otherwise, they are relatively free to decide when and where they will work, and how much time to devote to course preparation, grading papers and exams, study, research, and other activities. They may work staggered hours and teach classes at night and on weekends, particularly those faculty who teach older students who may have full-time jobs or family responsibilities on weekdays. They have even greater flexibility during the summer and school holidays, when they may teach or do research, travel, or pursue nonacademic interests.

Most colleges and universities have funds used to support faculty research or other professional development needs, including travel to conferences and research sites.

Part-time faculty generally spend little time on campus, since they usually don't have an office. In addition, they may teach at more than one college, requiring travel between their various places of employment.

Faculty may experience a conflict between their responsibilities to teach students and the pressure to do research. This may be a particular problem for young faculty seeking advancement. Increasing emphasis on undergraduate teaching performance, particularly at small liberal arts colleges, in tenure decisions may alleviate some of this pressure, however.

TRAINING

Most college and university faculty are in four academic ranks: professor, associate professor, assistant professor, and instructor. A small number are lecturers.

Most faculty members are hired as instructors or assistant professors. Four-year colleges and universities generally hire doctoral degree holders for full-time, tenure-track positions, but may hire master's degree holders or doctoral candidates for certain disciplines, such as the arts, or for part-time and temporary jobs.

Doctoral programs usually take 4 to 7 years of full-time study beyond the bachelor's degree. Candidates usually specialize in a subfield of a discipline, for example, organic chemistry, counseling psychology, or European history, but also take courses covering the whole discipline. Programs include 20 or more increasingly specialized courses and seminars plus comprehensive examinations on all major areas of the field. They also include a dissertation, a report on original research to answer some significant question in the field.

Students in the natural sciences and engineering usually do laboratory work; in the humanities, they study original documents and other published material. The dissertation, done under the guidance of one or more faculty advisors, usually takes one or two years of full-time work.

In some fields, particularly the natural sciences, some students spend an additional two years on postdoctoral research and study before taking a faculty position.

A major step in the traditional academic career is attaining tenure. Newly-hired faculty serve a certain period (usually 7 years) under term contracts. Then, their record of teaching, research, and overall contribution to the institution is reviewed;

tenure is granted if the review is favorable and positions are available. With tenure, a professor cannot be fired without just cause and due process. Those denied tenure usually must leave the institution. Tenure protects the faculty's academic freedom, the ability to teach and conduct research without fear of being fired for advocating unpopular ideas. It also gives both faculty and institutions the stability needed for effective research and teaching, and provides financial stability for faculty members. About 60 percent of full-time faculty are tenured, and many others are in the probationary period.

Some faculty, based on teaching experience, research, publication, and service on campus committees and task forces, move into administrative and managerial positions, such as departmental chairperson, dean, and president. At four-year institutions, such advancement requires a doctoral degree.

JOB OUTLOOK

Employment of college and university faculty is expected to increase about as fast as the average for all occupations through the year 2005 as enrollments in higher education increase. Many additional openings will arise as faculty members retire. Faculty retirements should increase significantly from the late 1990s through 2005 as a large number of faculty who entered the profession during the 1950s and 1960s reach retirement age at this time.

Enrollments increased in the early and mid-1980s despite a decline in the traditional college-age (18–24) population. This resulted from a higher proportion of 18- to 24-year-olds attending college, along with a growing number of part-time, female, and older students. Enrollments are expected to continue to grow through the year 2005, particularly as the traditional college-age population begins increasing after 1996, when the leading edge of the baby-boom echo generation (children of the baby boomers) reaches college age.

In the past two decades, keen competition for faculty jobs forced some applicants to accept part-time or short-term academic appointments that offered little hope of tenure, and others to seek nonacademic positions. This trend of hiring adjunct or part-time faculty should continue through the mid- to late-1990s due to financial difficulties universities and colleges are facing.

Many states have reduced funding for higher education. As a result, colleges increased the hiring of part-time faculty to save money on pay and benefits.

Once enrollments and retirements increase in the late 1990s, opportunities should improve for college faculty positions and for tenure, and fewer faculty should have to take part-time or short-term appointments.

Job prospects will continue to be better in certain fields such as business, engineering, health science, computer science, physical sciences, and mathematics, largely because very attractive nonacademic jobs will be available for many potential faculty.

Employment of college faculty also is related to the nonacademic job market through an echo effect. Excellent job prospects in a field—for example, computer science from the late 1970s to the mid-1980s—cause more students to enroll, increasing faculty needs in that field. On the other hand, poor job prospects in a field, such as history in recent years, discourages students and reduces demand for faculty.

SALARIES

Earnings vary according to faculty rank and type of institution and, in some cases, by field. Faculty in four-year institutions earn higher salaries, on the average, than those in two-year schools.

According to a 1992–93 survey by the American Association of University Professors, salaries for full-time faculty on 9-month contracts averaged $46,300. By rank, the average for professors was $59,500; associate professors, $44,100; assistant professors, $36,800; and instructors, $27,700. Those on 11- or 12-month contracts obviously earned more. In fields where there are high-paying nonacademic alternatives—notably medicine and law but also engineering and business, among others—earnings exceed these averages. In others—the fine arts, for example—they are lower.

Many faculty members have added earnings, both during the academic year and the summer, from consulting, teaching additional courses, research, writing for publication, or other employment.

Most college and university faculty enjoy some unique benefits, including access to campus facilities, tuition waivers for dependents, housing and travel allowances, and paid sabbatical leaves.

Part-time faculty have fewer benefits than full-time faculty.

RELATED FIELDS

College and university faculty function both as teachers and as researchers. They communicate information and ideas. Related occupations include elementary and secondary school teachers, librarians, writers, consultants, lobbyists, trainers and employee development specialists, and policy analysts. Faculty research activities often are similar to those of scientists, project managers, and administrators in industry, government, and nonprofit research organizations.

INTERVIEW

Jill Winland-Brown
Associate Professor, Florida Atlantic University

Jill Winland-Brown is a nurse _and_ a doctor—a doctor of education. She teaches future nurses at Florida Atlantic University in Boca Raton, Florida. She has been an R.N. for 25 years and a university professor for 15 years.

What's the Job Really Like?

"There are three components to my work: teaching, service, and research.

"I teach clinical and theory courses such as nursing ethics, leadership management, and technological skills (giving medications, starting IVs, etc.) 12 hours a week. In addition, there's preparing lessons and grading papers.

"The service part of my job means giving something back to the community and to the university. I serve on a lot of boards and committees. I advise undergraduate and graduate students and help them with independent studies or their theses or dissertations.

"When you're a professor you're expected to do research, to further your own knowledge and that of others in important areas. Some of my research topics have been 'problems for disabled nurses' and 'summer camp nursing.' You write papers to report what you've learned and you submit these papers to professional journals for publication.

"I do a little of each—teaching, service, research—in any one day.

"What I love most about my work, though, is watching my students learn and mature and then go on to find rewarding careers. I like working with a wide range of students, whether they're freshmen, seniors, or master's level students, or R.N.s coming back to earn their bachelor's degree. Every day you could see some of each; it's almost like seeing them grow in the same day.

"I'm an advisor to many students, too. They're assigned to me when they first begin and they stay with me all the way through. I like being able to follow them through their education and getting to know them well.

"I also enjoy being near people who are working in a variety of disciplines. Most hospital nurses work only with other health care professionals. In a university setting you come in contact with all different kinds of people.

"But we have to serve on a large number of committees. They take up a lot of time. And for university professors there's also the pressure of 'publish or perish.' You're expected to write articles and have them published in professional journals. You might spend a lot of time on two different papers; one gets published right away, the other you might have to submit several times, but they're both of equal value. It takes a lot of time."

How Jill Winland-Brown Got Started

"I started in a three-year diploma program and got my R.N. I worked for seven years and then went back to earn my bachelor's, then my master's, then my doctorate. I worked as a nurse throughout my studies."

Expert Advice

"These days it's much better to start out directly in a bachelor's program; it will take you less time. And though right now nurses all take the same licensing exam, in a few years that will change. There will be a technical level and a professional level exam and only the B.S.N. graduate will be at the professional level. If you want to teach, or even if you don't and you want to practice any other area of nursing, you should make sure you study for your bachelor's. It will be the entry into professional practice and will open many more doors for you."

● ● ●

INTERVIEW
Judy Burns
Adjunct Lecturer, UCLA

Judy Burns teaches screenwriting classes at UCLA Extension and in UCLA's MFA program. She has had an extensive career in television including writing for shows such as "Star Trek," "Mission Impossible," "The Fugitive," "Toma," "Vegas," "T.J. Hooker," "Marcus Welby M.D.," "Lucas Tanner," and "MacGyver."

She also teaches screenwriting on America Online. (See her interview in Chapter 3.)

What the Job's Really Like

"This year I taught a class at UC Riverside and Ithaca College in New York and at UCLA Extension and UCLA in the MFA program. Next year I'm hoping my load will increase at UC Riverside and the year after that it would be nice to be on a tenure track at the associate professor level. Nothing is definite yet.

"At UCLA Extension I teach Introduction to Screenwriting and Fixing Your Script, which is a rewrite class. I'll also be teaching 'Star Trek and the Craft of Screenwriting,' which is a specialty class I love to teach.

"I'm in the classroom 6 hours a week for the two classes. But then I also give office hours. I usually spend a few hours a week meeting with students. Then there's preparation and grading, so for a 3-hour class I probably put in double hours a week for it. But of course I only get paid for the actual classroom hours.

"Concurrently I am teaching a graduate course in the School of Theater, Film, and Television at UCLA and this class is a version of Fixing Your Script called Polishing Your Script.

"They called me over to teach this class because of my work in the Extension program. It's the first time they've ever had a rewrite class in the history of the program.

"I like the constant contact with the kids. I find that writers who work in a little room sometimes become too introspective and they don't maintain contact with humanity—which is what they need to write and talk about. The constant influx of new ideas is great—you absorb all of that.

"The only downside is that it takes time away from my own writing, that I have to set aside specific time to do my own work. But that's the only downside. I love the kids and they love me."

How Judy Burns Got Started

"I have a B.A. in anthropology from UC Irvine. Years later I went back for a master's at Cal State San Bernadino in 1989. It was an interdisciplinary major in theater, English, and history. Now I just finished my Ph.D. in critical studies in theater at UCLA.

"I came up through Hollywood as a story editor and producer—which means I was taught how to be these things and was taught by very good people. So basically I was on the other side of the desk every day dealing with writers who came to sell stories to me. I was passing on what I understood and I think probably in 1989 I suddenly said to myself—you know all this information, it's time to pass it on.

"But then I realized that in order to pass it on properly I would have to understand the roots of screenwriting. I had come into screenwriting through the back door. I became a screenwriter because basically I needed money. I was in school studying anthropology and I needed money for a ticket to Africa. I wanted to go dig bones.

"And here I was suddenly selling, then on staff. I was a writer, but I'd never had any academic training for it. I was a transplanted anthropologist. It's not a bad background, that and psychology, but I'd never had Shakespeare courses or drama or I had never read a Tennessee Williams play. But I had a knack for writing and I had read all my life.

"All my credits are in television. I broke in on 'Star Trek.' The show I wrote won an Emmy for special effects, it's called the 'Tholian Web.'

"I don't want to disillusion young people, but I had managed to work consistently for 20 years and then decided to go back to school and teach what I know. I'd rather be poor and refreshed, constantly in contact with students. There comes a time when you have to give it back and fill up your own container. After 20 years I felt depleted. By going back to school I had the time to read and then took teaching assistant positions and was suddenly in contact with young people and my universe expanded beyond just television. What I found was that the more I read, the more I absorbed, and I then almost immediately began to teach these things. I learned to appreciate teaching as an art form."

Expert Advice

"In order to become an instructor, you have to have a good long history of working in a particular profession or you need to get a degree, at least a master's or preferably a doctorate. You have to be willing to invest the time to do that. A bachelor's degree won't get you very far."

●   ●   ●

FOR MORE INFORMATION

Professional societies generally provide information on academic and nonacademic employment opportunities in their fields. You can find addresses for professional associations for many academic disciplines in the *Occupational Outlook Handbook*. Another resource is the *Encyclopedia of Associations*, available at your library.

For information about faculty union activities on two- and four-year college campuses, contact:

American Federation of Teachers
555 New Jersey Ave. NW
Washington, DC 20001

For information on college teaching careers, contact:

American Association of University Professors
12 14th St. NW
Washington, DC 20005

Special publications on higher education, available in libraries, list specific employment opportunities for faculty. The major periodical is the *Chronicle of Higher Education*.

5 Writers and Journalists

🎓 **EDUCATION**
B.A./B.S. Preferred

💲💲💲 **SALARY/EARNINGS**
$25,000 to $50,000

WRITERS

Writers share knowledge through the written word. They develop original fiction and nonfiction for books, magazines and trade journals, newspapers, technical reports, company newsletters, radio and television broadcasts, movies, and advertisements.

Writers first select a topic or are assigned one by an editor. Topics may be ideas, tangible objects, events, people, or organizations. Writers gather information through personal observation, library research, and interviews. Sometimes, they change the focus to a more interesting related topic as they learn more. They select and organize the material and put it into words that effectively convey it to the reader. Besides reporting the information they gather, they may analyze and interpret it. Writers often revise or rewrite sections, searching for the best organization of the material or just the right phrasing.

Newswriters prepare news items for newspapers or news broadcasts, based on information supplied by reporters or wire services.

Columnists analyze news and write columns or commentaries, based on personal knowledge and experience. Editorial writers write comments to stimulate or mold public opinion, in accordance with their publication's viewpoint.

Technical writers put scientific and technical information into readily understandable language. They prepare operating and maintenance manuals, catalogs, parts lists, assembly instructions, sales promotion materials, and project proposals. They also plan and edit technical reports and oversee preparation of illustrations, photographs, diagrams, and charts.

Copy writers write advertising copy for use by publication or broadcast media to promote the sale of goods and services.

Established writers may work on a freelance basis; they sell their work to publishers or publication units, manufacturing firms, and public relations and advertising departments or agencies. They sometimes contract to complete specific assignments such as writing about a new product or technique.

JOB OUTLOOK FOR WRITERS

Nearly a third of salaried writers work for newspapers, magazines, and book publishers. Substantial numbers also work in advertising agencies, in radio and television broadcasting, in public relations firms, and on journals and newsletters published by business and nonprofit organizations, such as professional associations, labor unions, and religious organizations. Others develop publications for government agencies or write for motion picture companies.

Many technical writers work for computer software firms or manufacturers of aircraft, chemicals, pharmaceuticals, and computers and other electronic equipment.

Jobs with major book publishers, magazines, broadcasting companies, advertising agencies and public relations firms, and the federal government are concentrated in New York, Chicago, Los Angeles, Boston, Philadelphia, San Francisco, and Washington, DC.

More widely dispersed throughout the country are jobs with newspapers; and professional, religious, business, technical, and trade union magazines or journals. Technical writers are employed throughout the country, but the largest concentrations are in the Northeast, Texas, and California.

Thousands of other persons work as freelancers earning some income from their articles, books, and, less commonly, television and movie scripts. Most support themselves primarily with income from other sources.

Employment of writers is expected to increase about as fast as the average for all occupations through the year 2005. Employment of salaried writers and editors by newspapers, periodicals, book publishers, and nonprofit organizations is expected to increase with growing demand for their publications. Growth of advertising and public relations agencies should also be a source of new jobs. Demand for technical writers is expected to increase because of the continuing expansion of scientific and technical information and the continued need to communicate it. Many job openings will also occur as experienced workers transfer to other occupations or leave the labor force. Turnover is relatively high in this occupation; many freelancers leave because they cannot earn enough.

Through the year 2005, the outlook for most writing jobs is expected to continue to be keenly competitive primarily because so many people are attracted to the field. However, opportunities will be good for technical writers because of the more limited number of writers who can handle technical material. Opportunities should be better on small dailies and weekly newspapers and in small radio and television stations, where the pay is low. Persons preparing to be writers should also have academic preparation in another field as well, either to qualify them as writers specializing in that field or to enter that field if they are unable to get a writing job.

TRAINING FOR WRITERS

A college degree generally is required. Although some employers look for a broad liberal arts background, most prefer to hire people with degrees in communications, journalism, or English.

Technical writing requires a degree in or some knowledge about a specialized field—engineering, business, or one of the sciences, for example. In many cases, people with good writing skills can pick up specialized knowledge on the job. Some transfer from jobs as technicians, scientists, or engineers. Some begin as research assistants, editorial assistants, or trainees in a technical information department, develop technical communication skills, and then assume writing duties.

High school and college newspapers, literary magazines, and community newspapers and radio and television stations all provide valuable but sometimes unpaid practical writing experience. Many magazines, newspapers, and broadcast stations have internships for students. Interns write short pieces, conduct research and interviews, and learn about the publishing or broadcasting business.

In small firms, beginning writers may not only work as editorial or production assistants but also write or edit material right away. They often advance by moving to other firms. In larger firms, jobs usually are structured more formally. Beginners generally do research, fact checking, or copy editing. They take on full-scale writing or editing duties less rapidly than do the employees of small companies. Advancement comes as they are assigned more important articles.

SALARIES FOR WRITERS

In 1992, beginning salaries for writers and editorial assistants averaged $20,000 annually, according to the Dow Jones Newspaper Fund. Those who had at least 5 years experience averaged more than $30,000, and senior editors at the largest newspapers earned over $60,000 a year.

According to the 1992 Technical Communicator's Salary Survey, median annual salaries for technical writers were as follows:

Entry level	$26,700
Mid-level nonmanagement	35,000
Mid-level management	40,000
Senior management	45,400

The average annual salary for technical writers and editors in the federal government in nonsupervisory, supervisory, and managerial positions was $40,669; other writers and editors averaged $39,077.

 **EDUCATION**
B.A./B.S. Required

$$$ SALARY/EARNINGS
$20,000 to $40,000

JOURNALISTS

Reporters and correspondents play a key role in our society. They gather information and prepare stories that inform us about local, state, national, and international events; present points of view on current issues; and report on the actions of public officials, corporate executives, special interest groups, and others who exercise power. In covering a story, they investigate leads and news tips, look at documents, observe on the scene, and interview people. Reporters take notes and may also take photographs or shoot videos. At their office, they organize the material, determine their focus or emphasis, write their stories, and may also edit videos. Many enter information or stories on portable computers, then submit it to their offices using a telephone modem. In some cases, newswriters write the story from information collected and submitted by the reporter.

General assignment reporters write up news as assigned, such as an accident, a political rally, the visit of a celebrity, or a company going out of business. Large newspapers and radio and television stations assign reporters to gather news at specific locations or beats, such as police stations or courts. They also have reporters specializing in fields such as health, politics, foreign affairs, sports, theater, consumer affairs, social events, science, business, and religion.

Investigative reporters cover stories that take many days or weeks of information gathering.

News correspondents are stationed in large U.S. and foreign cities to report on news occurring there.

Reporters on small publications cover all aspects of the news, and also may take photographs, write headlines, lay out pages, edit wire service copy, and write editorials. They also may solicit advertisements, sell subscriptions, and perform general office work.

The work of reporters and correspondents is usually hectic. They are under great pressure to meet deadlines.

Working hours vary. Reporters on morning papers often work from late afternoon until midnight. Those on afternoon or evening papers generally work from early morning until early or mid-afternoon.

Magazine reporters generally work during the day. Reporters may have to change their work hours to meet a deadline or to follow late-breaking developments. Their work may demand long hours, irregular schedules, and some travel.

TRAINING FOR JOURNALISTS

Most employers prefer people with a bachelor's degree in journalism, but some hire graduates with other majors. They look for experience on school newspapers or broadcasting stations and internships with news organizations. Large city newspapers and stations may also prefer candidates with a degree in a subject-matter specialty such as economics, political science, or business. Large newspapers and broadcasters also require a minimum of 3 to 5 years experience as a reporter.

Bachelor's degree programs in journalism are available in over 300 colleges. About three-fourths of the courses in a typical curriculum are in liberal arts; the remainder are in journalism. Journalism courses include introductory mass media, basic reporting and copy editing, history of journalism, and press law and ethics.

Those planning newspaper or magazine careers usually specialize in news-editorial journalism.

Many community and junior colleges offer journalism courses or programs; credits may be transferable to 4-year journalism programs.

A master's degree in journalism was offered by over 100 schools in 1992; about 20 schools offered a Ph.D. degree. Some graduate programs are intended primarily as preparation for news careers, while others prepare journalism teachers, researchers and theorists, and advertising and public relations workers.

High school courses in English, journalism, and social studies provide a good foundation. Useful college liberal arts courses include English with an emphasis on writing, sociology, political science, economics, history, and psychology. Courses in computer science, business, and speech are useful as well. Fluency in a foreign language is necessary in some jobs.

Reporters need good word-processing skills, and computer graphics and desktop publishing skills are useful. A knowledge of news photography is valuable for entry-level positions which are for combination reporter/camera operator or reporter/photographer.

Experience in a part-time or summer job or an internship with a news organization is important. The Dow Jones Newspaper Fund and newspapers, magazines, and broadcast news organizations offer summer reporting and editing internships. Work on high school and college newspapers and broadcasting stations, community papers, and Armed Forces publications also helps.

In addition, more than 3,000 journalism scholarships, fellowships, and assistantships were awarded to college journalism students by universities, newspapers, foundations, and professional organizations in 1990.

Experience as a stringer—a part-time reporter who is paid only for stories printed—is also helpful.

Reporters should be dedicated to providing accurate and impartial news. Accuracy is important both to serve the public and because untrue or libelous statements can lead to costly lawsuits. A nose for news, persistence, initiative, poise, resourcefulness, a good memory, and the physical stamina and emotional stability to deal with pressing deadlines, irregular hours, and sometimes dangerous assignments are important.

JOB OUTLOOK FOR JOURNALISTS

Employment of reporters and correspondents is expected to grow about as fast as the average for all occupations through the year 2005, spurred mainly by an anticipated increase in the number of small town and suburban daily and weekly newspapers. Little or no increase is expected in the number of big city dailies.

Most job openings will arise from the need to replace reporters and correspondents who leave the occupation. Turnover is relatively high in this occupation. Some find the work too stressful and hectic, or don't like the lifestyle and transfer to other occupations where their skills are valuable, especially public relations and advertising work. Others leave because they are unable to move up to better-paid jobs in bigger cities.

Competition for reporting jobs on large metropolitan newspapers and broadcast stations and on national magazines will continue to be keen. Small town and suburban newspapers will continue to offer better opportunities for beginners. Many openings arise on small publications as reporters become editors or reporters on larger publications or leave the field. Talented writers who can handle highly specialized scientific or technical subjects have an advantage.

SALARIES FOR JOURNALISTS

The Newspaper Guild negotiates with individual newspapers on minimum salaries for both starting reporters and those still on the job after 3 to 6 years. The median minimum salary for reporters was about $406 a week as of August 1, 1992. Ten percent of the contracts called for minimums of $300 or less; 10 percent, $567 or more. The median minimum weekly salary for reporters after 3 to 6 years on the job was about $654 a week. Ten percent of the contracts called for top minimums of $479 or less; 10 percent, $856 or more.

RELATED FIELDS

Writers and editors communicate ideas and information. Other communications occupations include newspaper reporters and correspondents, radio and television announcers, advertising and public relations workers, and teachers.

Reporters and correspondents must write clearly and effectively to succeed in their profession. Others for whom writing ability is essential include technical writers, advertising copy writers, public relations workers, educational writers, fiction writers, biographers, screen writers, and editors.

Journalism graduates have the background for work in such closely related fields as advertising and public relations and many take jobs in these fields. Other graduates accept sales, managerial, and other nonmedia positions, in many cases because it is difficult to find media jobs.

INTERVIEW
Jan Goldberg
Author and Freelance Writer

Jan Goldberg has a B.A. in education from Roosevelt University in Chicago. Her articles have seen print in over 200 publications including <u>Complete Woman, Opportunity Magazine, Chicago Parent</u> and the Pioneer Press group. She is the author of six books published by VGM Career Horizons: <u>Careers in Journalism, Opportunities in Horticulture Careers, Opportunities in Research and Development Careers, Opportunities in Entertainment Careers, Careers for Adventurous Types and Other Go-Getters</u> and <u>On the Job: Real People Working in Communications</u>. She is also co-developer of the On the Job series.

What the Job's Really Like

"I consider my job to be among the most interesting jobs you could find, especially since I write both articles and books in a variety of subject areas. I'm constantly researching new subjects and learning something new. I feel as if I'm an explorer venturing into new territory every time I approach a new topic.

"I certainly never get bored. Right now, for instance, I'm completing a career book, rewriting and revising a Camp Fire activity book, and I have three career articles I've already been assigned.

"This week I also attended a writers' conference, so that means my next project will be to follow up on the contacts I made with several magazine editors there. I'll be putting together my resume and published clips of my articles as samples of my writing.

"A typical day consists of doing many things: the actual writing; keeping in touch with editors; doing research—which might mean going out to the library or some other particular place; or phoning in inquiries about various things.

"Everything I do, I do with an eye to the future. What projects will I be working on in three months from now, in six months from now, even a year from now? So you're always planning and always at different stages with different projects all the time.

"The good part of all of this is that I can call my own shots and make my own schedule. The bad part is the same, because in order to meet your obligations and do a good job, you really do have to put in a lot of time. Some days could be 12-hour days and other days, depending on deadlines and how many projects you have going on, you might be able to take some time off.

"Because I work from a home office, I can work whenever I want—but of course, because the work is always there, I never quite get away from it.

"Also, as a freelancer, you're self-employed, basically running your own business. You have to send out bills, keep good records, have several filing systems, and of course you have to know how to market and sell yourself well. You're doing everything any small business person would do."

"What I like the most is the anticipation of new projects, new ideas, being allowed to be creative and doing new things. But writing is hard work—which a lot of people don't know, realize—and sometimes it isn't always a lot of fun.

"For me, though, the most difficult part is negotiating contracts and trying to collect money that's owed to me."

How Jan Goldberg Got Started

"Writing was always my first love. My grandfather was a bookbinder, so as a little girl my sister and brother and I would make trips to his workplace on weekends—which was a special treat. I was so enthralled by the excitement of it, with colored pages and scraps of paper and books that seemed to be piled up to the sky—and the smell of it. I can still remember it and I know that I made up my mind then I would do something with books and writing.

"I'm certified to teach K-12 and I taught for several years but still it was always the writing that interested me. I started with poetry, then did book reviews for a while.

"I thought about doing some educational writing and made contacts at Scott Foresman and Addison Wesley and then started doing projects for them. I was doing textbook projects and activity workbooks and more and more I decided I preferred the writing to the teaching.

"Then I contacted an educational publisher that did magazines and I began to write for *Modern Health* and particularly *Career World*. From there I went in two different directions. I started writing books for NTC and branched out to other publications as well.

"I really enjoyed teaching and it was a tough call for me, but I've established myself now and I'll stay with the writing. But it's a good combination though, writing and teaching."

Expert Advice

"You need to have a lot of projects going on at one time if you're going to make a living being a freelance writer. As a novice you have to be patient or you'll never make it otherwise. It's a slow process getting established. You have to pay your dues as in any other profession. You have to be persistent and it requires a lot of discipline. And you can't really expect too much too soon.

"I've never really figured out an hourly wage for myself, but writing in general is not a high-paying profession. If you want to really make tons of money, you'd probably want to choose another career. Before you think about quitting your day job, you need to be sure how much money you'll be able to make to support yourself."

● ● ●

INTERVIEW

Michael Malone
Photojournalist

Michael Malone received his bachelor's degree in photojournalism at San Jose State University in California in 1981. He is currently assistant director of photography at the Sun-Sentinel, a major newspaper in South Florida.

What the Job's Really Like

"Photojournalism is telling a story through pictures. And though it's a form of journalism in which photographs dominate over written copy, photojournalists need to have a strong journalism background, too. To accurately report the news, you should have a complete understanding of the subject. You need to be aware of what's happening in the world, to know what makes things tick and what makes them not tick. You could cover exciting stories, in a war zone for example, where there's a lot of peril. But being a Jack-of-all-trades is the main requirement. Most photojournalists working for both major and minor newspapers are expected to cover tamer stories, too. The gamut runs from food, to fashion, to spot news, to sports, to a wide range of human interest features.

"The most intriguing and at the same time the most terrifying subject I covered was Hurricane Andrew. Being from California, I was used to natural disasters along the line of earthquakes, which though equally destructive, are much less predictable than hurricanes.

"I spent the night of the hurricane at the newspaper's downtown headquarters in Fort Lauderdale, then at about six in the morning I went out with a reporter to view the aftermath. I thought I had seen Mother Nature's wrath before with earthquake damage, but nothing had prepared me for this.

"As I traveled south the level of destruction worsened. Seeing waterlines three feet up the side of the building, coming across boats sitting in the middle of the street, then later visiting where the brunt of the hurricane had hit, seeing all that damage from just the pure force of the wind—to witness it as both a citizen and a photojournalist was a powerful experience. It's nothing I'm in a hurry to experience again, but it was pretty amazing."

How Michael Malone Got Started

"My training is the same as anyone else in journalism school; I had to take writing courses, too, but my concentration was in photojournalism.

"I also participated in several internships. This way I was able to make more contacts and have a better chance of lining up full-time employment when I graduated. At the same time I added to my portfolio and was able to create impressive specifics to include on my resume."

Expert Advice

"Photojournalism is highly competitive, so having a good education is very important. You have to work hard, get good grades, make contacts, and be one hundred percent committed to your career. Most photojournalists have at least a bachelor's degree, many, especially those with management inclinations, have a master's.

"There are a few different routes to take in the job-hunting process, but they all include putting together a professional portfolio.

"Some photojournalists identify the papers they would like to work for, and, at their own expense, fly out on spec to talk to the different editors—even when they know there are currently no openings. This approach, though a bit costly for someone just starting out, can often work. The job applicant makes himself known, and when an opening does occur, potential employers will remember your eager smile and top-quality portfolio.

"But I think job hunting through the mail is just as effective. Send out your portfolio with a good cover letter and don't be afraid to mention any story ideas you might have. Newspapers aren't looking for robots, they appreciate a photojournalist who does more than stand behind the camera and click his shutter.

"Then don't forget to follow up. I've made up my own picture postcards, using my best work. This helps to jog the editor's memory—and shows how creative you are."

• • •

FOR MORE INFORMATION

Writing

American Society of Journalists and Authors
1501 Broadway
New York, NY 10036

For information on college internships in magazine editing, contact:

American Society of Magazine Editors
575 Lexington Ave.
New York, NY 10022

For information on careers in technical writing, contact:
Society for Technical Communication, Inc.
901 N. Stuart St, Suite 304
Arlington, VA 22203

Journalism

Career information, including pamphlets titled *Facts about Newspapers* and, *Newspaper: What's in It for Me?*, are available from:

Newspaper Association of America
The Newspaper Center
Box 17407
Dulles International Airport
Washington, DC 20041

Newspaper Association of America Foundation
11600 Sunrise Valley Dr.
Reston, VA 22091

Information on careers in journalism, colleges and universities that offer degree programs in journalism or communications, and journalism scholarships and internships may be obtained from:

The Dow Jones Newspaper Fund, Inc.
P.O. Box 300
Princeton, NJ 08543-0300

For a list of junior and community colleges offering programs in journalism, contact:

Community College Journalism Association
San Antonio College
1300 San Pedro Ave.
San Antonio, TX 78212-4299

Information on union wage rates for newspaper and magazine reporters is available from:

The Newspaper Guild
Research and Information Department
8611 Second Ave.
Silver Spring, MD 20910

For a list of schools with accredited programs in their journalism departments, send a stamped, self-addressed envelope to:

Accrediting Council on Education in Journalism and Mass
    Communications
University of Kansas School of Journalism
Stauffer-Flint Hall
Lawrence, KS 66045

For general information about careers in journalism, contact:

Association for Education in Journalism and Mass
    Communication
University of South Carolina
1621 College St.
Columbia, SC 29208-0251

A pamphlet titled *A Career in Newspapers* can be obtained from:

National Newspaper Association
1627 K St. NW, Suite 400
Washington, DC 20006

Names and locations of newspapers and a list of schools and
departments of journalism are published in the *Editor and Publisher International Year Book*, available in most public libraries
and newspaper offices.

The NPPA (National Press Photographers Association) is an
organization that can help in the job hunt. They run a Job Information Bank and have regional and national divisions for professionals, students, and minorities. They invite photojournalists to write for membership information.

National Press Photographers Association
3200 Cloasdaile Drive, Suite 306
Durham, NC 27705

6 Radio and Television Reporters and Broadcasters

EDUCATION
B.A./B.S. Required
Other

$$$ SALARY/EARNINGS
$13,000 to $45,000

OVERVIEW

Radio and television reporters and broadcasters often compose stories and report live from the scene. Later, they may tape a commentary in the studio.

Announcers and newscasters are well-known personalities to radio and television audiences. Radio announcers, often called disk jockeys, select and introduce recorded music; present news, sports, weather, and commercials; interview guests; and report on community activities and other matters of interest to their audience. If a written script is required, they may do the research and writing. They often ad-lib much of the commentary. They also may operate the control board, sell commercial time to advertisers, and write commercial and news copy.

Announcers at large stations usually specialize in sports or weather, or in general news, and may be called newscasters or anchors. Some are news analysts. In small stations, one announcer may do everything.

News anchors, or a pair of co-anchors, present news stories and introduce in-depth videotaped news or live transmissions from on-the-scene reporters. Weathercasters, also called weather reporters or meteorologists, report and forecast weather conditions. They gather information from national satellite weather services, wire services, and other local and regional weather bureaus. Sportscasters select, write, and deliver the sports news. This may include interviews with sports personalities and live coverage of games played.

Broadcast news analysts, called commentators, present news stories and also interpret them and discuss how they may affect the nation or listeners personally.

Show hosts and hostesses interview guests about their lives, their work, or topics of current interest. They may ask questions of contestants, or manage play of games to enable contestants to win prizes.

Announcers frequently participate in community activities. Sports announcers, for example, are masters of ceremonies at touchdown club banquets or are on hand to greet customers at openings of sporting goods stores.

TRAINING

Entry to this occupation is highly competitive. While formal training in broadcast journalism from a college or technical school (private broadcasting school) is valuable, station officials pay particular attention to taped auditions that show an applicant's delivery and in television appearance and style on commercials, news, and interviews. Those hired by television stations usually start out as production secretaries, production assistants, researchers, or reporters and are given a chance to move into announcing if they show an aptitude for on-air work. Newcomers to TV broadcasting also may begin as news camera operators.

A beginner's chance of landing an on-air newscasting job is remote, except possibly for a small radio station. In radio, newcomers generally start out taping interviews and operating equipment.

Announcers usually begin at a station in a small community and, if qualified, may then move to a better-paying job in a large city. Announcers also may advance by hosting a regular program as a disc jockey, sportscaster, or other specialist. In the national networks, competition for jobs is particularly intense, and employers look for college graduates with at least several years of successful announcing experience.

High school courses in English, public speaking, drama, foreign languages, and electronics are valuable, and hobbies such as sports and music are additional assets. Students may gain valuable experience at campus radio or TV facilities and at commercial stations.

Some stations and cable systems offer financial assistance and on-the-job training in the form of internships, apprentice programs, co-op work programs, scholarships, or fellowships.

Persons considering enrolling in a broadcasting school should contact personnel managers of radio and television stations as well as broadcasting trade organizations to determine the school's reputation for producing suitably trained candidates.

JOB OUTLOOK

Radio and television announcers and newscasters held about 56,000 jobs in 1992. Nearly all were staff announcers, but some were freelance announcers who sold their services for individual assignments to networks and stations, or to advertising agencies and other independent producers.

Employment of announcers is expected to increase about as fast as the average for all occupations through the year 2005 as new radio and television stations are licensed and the number of cable television systems continues to grow. Most openings in this relatively small field will arise from the need to replace those who transfer to other kinds of work or leave the labor force. Many announcers leave the field because they cannot advance to better-paying jobs.

Competition for jobs as announcers will be very keen because the broadcasting field typically attracts many more job seekers than there are jobs. Small radio stations are more inclined to hire beginners, but the pay is low. Because competition for ratings is so intense in major metropolitan areas, large stations will continue to seek announcers and newscasters who have proven that they can attract and retain a large audience.

Newscasters who are knowledgeable in such areas as business, consumer, and health news may have an advantage over others. While specialization is more common at larger stations and the networks, many smaller stations also encourage it.

Employment in this occupation is not significantly affected by downturns in the economy. If recessions cause advertising revenues to fall, stations tend to cut behind-the-scenes workers rather than announcers and broadcasters.

SALARIES

Salaries in broadcasting vary widely. They are higher in television than in radio, higher in larger markets than in small ones, and higher in commercial than in public broadcasting.

According to a survey conducted by the National Association of Broadcasters and the Broadcast Cable Financial Management Association, the median salary for experienced radio announcers was $17,000 a year in 1992. Salaries ranged from $13,000 in the smallest markets to $45,000 in the largest markets for on-air personalities. News announcers' median was $17,700, ranging from $14,700 in the smallest to $40,330 in the largest markets. Sports reporters' median was $18,000, ranging from $12,500 in the smallest to $30,600 in the largest markets.

Among television announcers, news anchors' median salary was $41,000, ranging from $28,000 in the smallest to $163,000 in the largest markets. Weathercasters' median was $36,660, ranging from $25,200 to $103,321. Sportscasters' median was $31,900, ranging from $22,000 to $142,500.

Annual median salaries of radio reporters ranged from $12,000 in the smallest stations to $33,388 in the largest stations in 1992, according to a survey conducted by the National Association of Broadcasters. For all stations, the median salary was $16,000. Salaries of television reporters ranged from $16,052 in the smallest stations to $69,500 in the largest ones. For all stations, the median salary was $21,825.

RELATED FIELDS

The success of announcers and news broadcasters depends upon how well they speak to their audiences. Others for whom oral communication skills are vital are interpreters, sales workers, public relations specialists, teachers, and actors.

INTERVIEW

Lee Rodgers
Talk Show Host, KGO Radio, San Francisco

Lee Rodgers worked his way from a small "tea kettle" station in Tennessee back in 1959 (WHBG, Memphis—the station that launched Elvis Presley) to K G O Radio, San Francisco, which holds the number one spot in the West. Other major stations he has worked at include WIND, Chicago; WGSB, Miami; and KSD, St. Louis.

What the Job's Really Like

"I do a three-hour daily talk program on ABC's KGO in San Francisco, heard from Alaska to Mexico. The program takes three hours; the preparation—mostly extensive reading and planning programs—takes ten hours a day or more.

"Every day's a challenge, because the news—the basis for my program's content—changes daily. But the rewards are, (1) financial, because the skills required are far above those needed to play records and do an occasional joke and, (2) prestige, at least locally, because one is viewed as a person of influence, even by major office-holders.

"Plus, as the cliche' goes, while the hours may be long, the work is indoors, and there's no heavy lifting!

"But hours of daily phone contact with the public means that you spend a certain amount of your life trying to be civil to people you'd rather shoot if they tried to actually enter your home!

"And the penalty for failure—as defined by the ratings—is unemployment."

How Lee Rodgers Got Started

"I came from a very poor background, and when I was 13 I lost a substantial part of my right leg in a sawmill accident.

"I realized then that my options were somewhat limited. The day I graduated from high school my father gave me $40, which was all the money he had, and a bus ticket and said 'Son, good luck, this is what there is and this is all there is.'

"I thought broadcasting was maybe something I *could* do, given my handicap. I knew I had to do something, I had to work and I had to succeed.

"When I started out I had no knowledge of how the broadcasting industry worked. I took the usual route for a great many young men. I was a sports fanatic. I assumed that I could do a sportscasting job, at least as well as some of the people I heard on the radio, not realizing that there were probably a million other young guys my age with the same idea.

"I was good enough at it to get a job, and eventually ended up working major college sports across the country.

"I didn't realize how competitive it was until I was established at larger radio stations where I'd see this constant parade of young people coming in applying for jobs. Every day the mail would bring a big stack of audition tapes that accumulated on the program director's desk. Eventually I was in that position and they came pouring in to me.

"If I'd known how tough and competitive the broadcasting business was I'd probably have never even *tried* it. But, by the time I found out the odds against succeeding were overwhelming ... I was already successful!"

Expert Advice

"Strictly speaking, a college degree is not necessary. But I would recommend college to anybody because you're much more likely to come out a well-rounded person with more areas of knowledge than otherwise.

"As far as courses of study, there are a *few* colleges and universities offering worthwhile programs in broadcasting. However, most take an 'ivory-tower' approach that bears no resemblance to real-world radio and television. As a manager, I usually found that applicants from those schools were 'projects,' to be broken of bad habits before real learning could take place.

"Political science isn't a bad major but, frankly, I think history is more important to this kind of work than anything else you can study.

"But, far more important whether you go to college or not is that you have an insatiable curiosity about all sorts of topics and be an omnivorous reader. You also have to have the ability to formulate opinions on both sides of any topic and explain and defend them lucidly and articulately. And, it helps to have an entertainer's instinct for performing.

"After you get a foot in the door, get any opportunity you can to be on the air, even if it means 2:00 a.m. on Sundays.

"Then start taping yourself, critiquing yourself—and asking other people to critique you. Save the best of your tapes and keep updating them. (What sounds the best this year, I assure you, will not sound like your best next year. If it does, you're not making any progress.)

"A young person trying to get ahead in the business should always have an updated audition tape. If you hear of an opening or want to start pitching a bigger station in a bigger city down the road, have it ready for when you get the opportunity to talk to the program director.

"Show a track record of what you've done lately. We look for a background of successful performance on successful radio stations. Everyone loves a winner.

"And, be prepared to relocate. My career has been a model of stability compared to most broadcasters. Generally, moving up means moving out. Broadcasters in the know would say, 'You can always tell how good he is by the size of his U-Haul trailer.'

"Usually, if you're under any kind of contractual arrangement in your present city, they'll have a 'no-compete' clause in the local market that's fairly standard. And it's understandable. If they build you into a significant factor in the radio market, they don't want that expense and effort to be rewarded by having you go across the street to work for the competition.

"Learn to debate. Learn history and follow current events and learn to interpret 'the story behind the story.'

"Read extensively, discuss issues, seek fresh insights and remember—always—that broadcasting is a *business*. This doesn't mean 'selling out' one's views, but being aware that, whatever your views, you have to attract an audience or nobody gets paid.

"And if fierce competition and the necessity to pursue your work with unbelievable tenacity intimidate you ... do something else!"

"I think one of the best ways to learn how the business operates is, while you are going to school, try to get an internship at a major radio station. Many large stations have intern programs that give students an opportunity to earn zero while learning how the station works. (However, what you learn in that big station may have little relationship to what goes on in the small station—and the small station is probably where you'll get your first meager paycheck.)

"We offer internships at KGO. And some of our interns who are not headed directly for on-the-air work, but other jobs in the radio station, have been hired as a direct result of their internship here.

"But if you're looking for air work, the internship simply lets you know how the business operates so you walk in with some understanding of what goes on in a radio station.

"And, if you are going after on-the-air work, for almost everybody that means you're going to have to start either in small stations in small markets or small stations in big markets.

"Spots are competitive. If two applicants had the same qualifications the interview would probably be the most crucial.

"Presence is important. But these days, there isn't nearly as much emphasis on having that well-modulated voice in broadcasting, as was the case 20 or 30 years ago, especially doing this kind of radio.

"What you have to say is far more important than how you sound saying it. That doesn't mean that a voice that takes paint off the walls would be acceptable."

● ● ●

INTERVIEW
Al Sunshine
Television Investigative Reporter, Miami

Al Sunshine is a familiar face throughout South Florida. He is perhaps best known for his "Shame on You" reports seen on WCIX, Channel 6, the CBS affiliate in Miami.

What the Job's Really Like

"'Shame on You' is an investigative consumer action franchise for the station. We basically look at government incompetence, pollution, unscrupulous business practices, and we try to personalize the stories for people who are involved. After a lot of investigation and a lot of careful writing and production, we let people literally shake their fingers and say 'Shame On You' to the bad guys.

"Our investigations have been shown extensively throughout the state and I've been asked to testify in some state committees. I've lost track of how many laws we've gotten on the books as a result of our stories.

"I think the stories that have had the most impact have been those on car repair fraud and scams. We showed frustrations of consumers who were ripped off by unscrupulous mechanics. Not only do we have car repair regulations in Dade and Broward counties as a result of our stories, but we now have a statewide car repair protection law for consumers.

"The story that most affected me personally was something that happened 20 years ago—two kids who were abducted at gunpoint from a church ice cream social. We heard about it Monday morning and about an hour after that we got reports that two bodies had been found. As I was interviewing the police, a stranger next to me collapsed in tears. His son had been missing and when he heard that the police were at a crime scene he hurried over to find out what was happening. As it turned out, his son was one of the victims.

"It was absolutely a gut-wrenching occurrence to have someone listening in on the interview and then collapse when he realized it had been his son who'd been murdered.

"I cite this as a way of illustrating that this is not a career that you are going to be working nine to five and walking away from. You'll be dancing in and out of other people's tragedies and it will take a toll on you. It absolutely will."

How Al Sunshine Got Started

"As far back as high school, I had a great curiosity about what was going on about me and I started writing and taking pictures for the high school paper. I was curious not only about the events that were happening, but I wanted to look deeper, to get under the surface and to find out why they were happening. Why some systems that were there to protect us weren't working, perhaps.

"From high school, I went to the University of Miami. That was in 1968. I started off in marine biology, from there went to psychology and from there into mass communications. Like many kids, I bounced around a lot. I graduated in 1972 with a major in psychology and communications.

"The interesting thing for me during that time, in 1968, 1969, and 1970, was that it was during the era of social and political confrontation and campus activism. There was Watergate and Kent State. I literally went from being a student at the University of Miami, working for the university newspaper covering campus politics and campus news to Watergate, Kent State, and tear gas at the Democratic and Republican conventions in 1972. I cut my teeth working television on some very important issues.

"Miami back in the 1960s and 1970s had a huge national reputation. We got involved in a lot of stories—anti-Castro militants, drug dealers, refugees, and political intrigue. A lot of other prominent investigative reporters have come out of Miami. Brian Ross worked in Miami for quite a long time; John Scott of 'Dateline' was based here. Today, Miami still has a national reputation for investigative journalism.

"I started working with WTVJ, which was the CBS affiliate at the time, and for 12 or 13 years I covered a lot of great stories. Then I went to work for CNN in about 1983. I covered the space shuttle, and *Challenger*, and space program problems at NASA. I also got involved covering the Contras behind enemy lines for CNN in Nicaragua. I was also covering the covert airline supply operation for the Contras that was based out of South Florida.

"I went back to work for CBS in 1989 and got volunteered for the 'Shame on You' spot. I've also been on 'Geraldo' three or four times covering some national stories. We exposed scams against women—diet and health fraud, and stories on modeling agency scams and the dark side of the modeling industry, exposing these agencies that scam young girls into paying thousands of dollars with the promise of a career that never materializes.

"I was also on 'Geraldo' with an investigation I'd done into unsanitary school cafeterias. That investigation was shown in the Florida legislature and I'm proud to say resulted in new disclosure laws requiring schools to post their health inspections.

Expert Advice

"You cannot take no for an answer from either a prospective employer or someone you're trying to talk to as a source on a story. It's the kind of work that no one is going to help you with. It's something you have to have burning inside you, an incredible desire to want to do this in the light of a lot of adversity.

"It's much more than a job, it's almost a lifestyle. You need the ability to keep your eyes and ears open for possible stores and the ability to hear a lot of people's tragedies and put them into prospective. You have to try to make a positive change come from it all.

"I think there's a responsibility with journalists that is being recognized more and more. You can't simply walk away from a story after showing the problem. You also have to show the other side and give your viewers or readers a perspective on why things are happening. You have to offer a possible answer and a possible way of trying to prevent future problems.

"Journalism, for the most part, is very good at tearing down institutions and tearing down politicians. But in all fairness, you owe your viewers and readers some answers.

"How should you prepare yourself? Within the news business it's very controversial whether you should study journalism or whether you should get an all-around education in liberal arts. That's something everybody has to decide for themselves, but I'd caution you that the world out there does not revolve around journalism. It revolves around families, work, education, and history. You can't be a good reporter unless you can write a good sentence, unless you understand economics, unless you understand local government. A liberal arts education will help you to become a well-rounded individual."

● ● ●

FOR MORE INFORMATION

For a list of schools that offer programs and courses in broadcasting, contact:

Broadcast Education Association
1771 N St. NW
Washington, DC 20036

For information on FCC licenses, write to:

Federal Communications Commission
1919 M St. NW
Washington, DC 20552

General information on the broadcasting industry is available from:
National Association of Broadcasters
1771 N St. NW
Washington, DC 20036

For information on careers in broadcast news, contact:

Radio-Television News Directors Association
1717 K St. NW, Suite 615
Washington, DC 20006

Museum Workers

🎓 **EDUCATION**
B.A./B.S. Required
Postgraduate Preferred

💲💲💲 **SALARY/EARNINGS**
Varies—See Charts
(pages 93-94)

OVERVIEW

Almost all museums provide some sort of educational programming for the public, providing a variety of opportunities for those wanting work that allows them to share knowledge. Educators and program developers design classes, workshops, lectures, and tours and often offer outreach programs to the schools or local community in which they are located.

Today, there are as many different kinds of museums as the items they display or the topics they explain. Some are famous establishments, such as those that the Smithsonian Institution comprises; others are small enterprises, known only locally.

Art Museums

Art museums are buildings where objects of aesthetic value are preserved and displayed. Art museums have a variety of functions including acquiring, conserving, and exhibiting works of art; providing art education for the general public; and conducting art historical research.

History Museums

From acquiring collections and preserving them, to explaining and displaying them, in history museums dedicated professionals have the chance to work with every aspect of the relics and other forms of physical evidence of the past. History museums can cover a particular period, such as Colonial America, or a particular topic, such as entertainment or advertising. A history museum's collection could be displayed in a modern building constructed specifically for that purpose, or the building itself, along with its contents, could be the museum. Examples include the homes of famous people such as Paul Revere or Thomas Jefferson, or historic structures such as lighthouses or old courthouses.

Living History Museums

A living history museum is a vibrant, active village, town, or city where the day-to-day life of a particular time period has been authentically recreated. The houses and public buildings are restored originals or thoroughly researched reproductions. Interiors are outfitted with period furniture, cookware, bed linens, and tablecloths.

Employees known as character interpreters function as residents, wearing the clothing of their day and discussing their dreams and concerns with visitors as they go about their daily tasks. If you were to stop a costumed gentleman passing by and ask where the nearest McDonald's is, for example, he wouldn't have any idea what you were talking about—unless he thought to direct you to a neighbor's farm. He might even do so using the dialect of his home country.

Colonial Williamsburg in Virginia and Plimoth Plantation in Massachusetts are just two examples of living history museums. These large enterprises offer employment for professional and entry-level workers in a wide variety of categories.

Natural History Museums

Natural history museums are dedicated to research, exhibition, and education in the natural sciences. Museums vary in size and collections and could include all or some of the following departments: anthropology, astronomy, botany, entomology, fossil and living vertebrates, geology, herpetology and ichthyology, mammalogy, mineralogy, ornithology, and vertebrate paleontology.

Collections could include artifacts from ancient civilizations, gems and jewels, fossils, meteorites, and animals from around the world displayed in lifelike settings.

Science Museums and Discovery Centers

Science museums preserve and display objects that have been important to the development of science and technology. Science centers, or discovery centers, as they are sometimes called, generally teach the principles related to these fields. They often involve visitors in hands-on activities, many catering particularly to children. The two types of science museums are not necessarily mutually exclusive, although most institutions fall into one category or the other.

Planetariums

Planetariums are structures, usually with dome ceilings, that are outfitted to give audiences the illusion of being outside under a starlit sky. Through the use of projectors, slides, movies, and computers the location of the planets and stars and all other sorts of astronomical activity can be demonstrated.

Planetariums are often part of a science museum complex, with most large cities now having full-scale facilities. They are used as tourist and educational attractions with elaborate space exhibits or public observational facilities. Smaller planetariums are also associated with universities and are used for classroom instruction in geography, navigation, and astronomy.

National Monuments

National monuments, such as the Statue of Liberty and Ellis Island, are operated by the National Park Service, which falls under the umbrella of the U.S. Department of the Interior. These federally funded museums offer a wide range of full-time and seasonal employment for interpretive rangers and other personnel.

Preservation Boards and Historical Societies

The mission of most preservation boards and historical societies is to preserve, protect, defend, and promote the cultural, social, economic, environmental, and architectural integrity of their particular district or historic site.

Preservation boards and historical societies offer full-time employment or volunteer opportunities for many educational positions. These include (but are not limited to) archivists (see Chapter 8), researchers, curators, and information officers.

Many boards and societies are membership-funded; others might receive government or private grants to carry on their work. The better-funded operations are able to hire specialists to work in their particular fields. Boards and societies with limited funds rely heavily on professionals willing to volunteer their time. The few paid employees take on a variety of tasks crossing career categories.

Other Museums

Museums deal with tangible objects, both inanimate and animate. In addition to the museums just listed, other categories also exist. The American Association of Museums (AAM) includes arboreta and botanic gardens and zoos and aquariums in their definition of what a museum is.

Other museums cover only a specific item, event, or phenomenon or cater to a particular audience. The Rock 'n' Roll Museum in Cleveland, the Holocaust Museum in Washington, DC, the Teddy Bear Museum in Fort Myers, Florida, and museums developed specifically for children are examples of these.

Jobs within Museums

Professional job classifications within museums fall into several categories; those most related to sharing knowledge include collections, curation, education and interpretation, and research.

Many job titles are common to each kind of museum, but the job description will vary depending on the institution. Curators, for example, are found in almost every kind of museum, from art to science and history museums, even though the collections they deal with and their specific duties are very different. Researchers could work in planetariums or in living history museums. Presenters, character interpreters, and tour guides could work in living history museums or for historical societies.

The professionals interviewed in this chapter work in the following positions:

Education coordinator

Researcher

Character interpreter

Curator

Director of special projects

TRAINING

With museums offering so many diverse careers, it stands to reason that avenues of training leading to these professions would be equally diverse. A tour guide would have a background different from a researcher, an educator's preparation would differ from a curator's.

In addition, different museums often look for different qualifications. Some prefer candidates to have an advanced degree or certificate in museology or museum studies. Others expect to hire professionals with strong academic concentrations in, for example, astronomy, history, or anthropology. Most are impressed with a combination of academic and hands-on training earned through internships or volunteer programs.

There are, however, several skills and personal traits common to all museum professionals. For a start, all museum workers need to have excellent interpersonal skills. Educators, character interpreters, and tour guides present information to staff and visitors, and directors and curators supervise staff and cultivate contacts with donors and other community members. The ability to get along with others and to work well as a team is a vital asset in museum work.

Of equal importance is the ability to communicate through the written word. Museums meet their missions with their collections of objects, but to do so, museum workers must have strong writing skills. Good written language skills show themselves in grant applications, exhibition catalogs, brochures, administrative and scholarly reports, training and educational materials, legal agreements, interpretive labeling for exhibits, object records, and much more.

How you proceed will depend upon your interests and circumstances. If you are clear from the start what avenue you wish to pursue, you can tailor-make a course of study for yourself at the university of your choosing. Courses you'll take or the degree toward which you'll work will depend in part on whether you are a new student or you are already a museum professional making a mid-career change.

Traditionally, new hires to the field of museum work have completed a bachelor's and master's degree in academic disciplines appropriate to the intended career. Curators for art museums have studied art and art history; curators for natural history museums have studied biology, anthropology, archeology, and so on. And while such a background still serves as the main foundation for successful museum work, for the last thirty years or so more and more people have explored university programs offering practical and theoretical training in the area of museum studies. Courses such as museum management, curatorship, fundraising, exhibition development, and law and museums offer a more specific approach to the work at hand. This, coupled with a broad background in liberal arts or specialization in an academic discipline provides the museum professional with a knowledge base better designed to serve the needs of the museum.

Whatever your course of study, these days most museums require an upper-level degree, either in an academic discipline or in museum studies, museum science, or museology. Also required is an intensive internship or record of long-term volunteer work.

Career Tracks

What follows are three possible tracks with which a student can proceed to prepare for a career in museums:

Track One

Bachelor's degree in general museum studies, museology, or museum science

Master's degree or doctorate in a specific academic discipline

Internship arranged through the university or directly with a museum in a particular field

Track Two

Bachelor's degree in liberal arts or a specific academic discipline

Master's degree or certificate in museum studies, museology, or museum science

Internship arranged through the university or directly with a museum in a particular field

Track Three (for the museum professional changing careers or upgrading skills)

Master's degree or certificate in museum studies, *or*

Non-credit-bearing certificate in museum studies (short-term course)

The internship is considered the most crucial practical learning experience and is generally a requirement in all programs. The internship can run from ten weeks to a year with varying time commitments per week.

Volunteering and Internships

Although formal academic training is vital to your resume, hands-on experience is of equal importance. Not only does it provide a host of significant skills, it also allows the career explorer to make an informed decision about the suitability of museum work. A person who starts with a term of volunteer work, even before beginning a college program, will have a better idea of what career options museums have to offer and whether these options are right for him or her.

Many museums rely heavily on volunteer energy and can place volunteers in almost every museum department, from tour guide and gift shop sales to assisting curators and exhibit designers.

The easiest way to volunteer your time is to call a museum and ask to speak to the volunteer coordinator. He or she will work with you to match your interests with the museum's needs.

Volunteer programs are usually flexible about the number of hours and days per week they expect from their volunteers.

Most academic museum studies programs require an internship before a degree or certificate can be awarded. In addition, many museums have their own internship programs that are offered to full-time students as well as recent graduates. You can check with your university department first to see what arrangements they traditionally make. If the burden is on you to arrange an internship, either during your academic program or after you've graduated, contact the museum's internship coordinator. If the museum has no formal internship program, talk first to a museum staff member to determine where there might be a need. Then, you can write a proposal incorporating your interests in a department where help will be appreciated.

Internships can be either paid or unpaid and are usually a more formal arrangement than volunteering. The number of hours and weeks will be structured and the intern might be expected to complete a specific project during his or her time there. Often, college credit can be given.

The AAM has published a resource report called *Standards and Guidelines for Museum Internships*. It covers what museums expect from their interns and what interns can and should expect from the museum. It is available through AAM's bookstore, whose address is at the end of this chapter.

Later, when it comes time to job hunt, a successful internship or stint of volunteer work can open the door at the training institution or at other museums.

JOB OUTLOOK

Each year more and more historic buildings are nominated for inclusion on the National Register. Many of these sites are operated as historic house museums open to the public. This means that more and more employment opportunities are opening up for museum workers.

But history museums are not the only depositories expanding across the country. Art galleries and art museums can be found in almost any town; science museums, discovery centers, and planetariums are maintained in most mid- to large-size cities or university towns.

New job titles have been added to the list once limited to curators and librarians. The field of museum work is now open to all sorts of professionals, including restoration specialists, designers, planners, financiers, audience advocates, information specialists and many more.

Although the competition in some sectors is stiff, and funding always seems to lag behind public demand, a persistent job seeker can get his or her foot in the door through volunteering or participating in a student internship. The majority of professionals interviewed in the pages to come report that the first step to landing their job was, indeed, a stint of volunteering or interning.

Employment of curators is expected to increase about as fast as the average for all occupations through the year 2005. Although the rate of turnover among curators is relatively low, the need to replace workers who leave the occupation or stop working will create some additional job openings.

Museums and botanical and zoological gardens, where curators are concentrated, are expected to grow in response to increased public interest in science, art, history, and technology.

Despite the anticipated increase in the employment of curators, competition for jobs is expected to be keen. A job as a curator is attractive to many people, and many have the necessary subject knowledge; yet there are only a few openings. Consequently, candidates may have to work part time, or as an intern, or even as a volunteer assistant curator or research associate after completing their formal education, and substantial work experience in collection management, exhibit design, or restoration will be necessary for permanent status. Job opportunities for curators should be best in art and history museums, since these are the largest employers in the museum industry.

SALARIES

Salaries within museums vary by type of museum, by position, by the region of the country in which the museum is located, and by the funding each museum has to work with. In general, museum salaries are not particularly high.

Art Museums

The Association of Art Museum Directors annually conducts a salary survey of both current and former AAMD members. In the 1994 survey, from which the following figures are reported, 181 of the 215 art museums surveyed responded—a response rate of 85 percent.

The salaries reported in the survey were for professional positions that were likely to be filled nationally, rather than locally. The survey provides characteristics of responding museums and lists salaries by size of budget and region.

The table that follows excerpts salary information from the 1994 survey for all responding museums. To obtain the latest annual survey contact either the Association of Art Museum Directors or the American Association of Museums. Both addresses are listed at the end of this chapter.

Salaries within Natural History Museums

Salaries at natural history museums tend to be less than at art museums.

Here are the salary ranges for the different job titles at Carnegie Museum of Natural History. These figures should be used only as a guide. Keep in mind that salaries will vary according to the region of the country and the size of the institution's budget.

Interns—Paid internships usually offer $15,000 per year.

Educators—The average is in the high twenties. The top educator chairman would earn around $40,000 a year.

Salaries in Art Museums

Position	Lowest Salary	Highest Salary	Mean Salary	No. of Museums Reporting
Director	$45,000	$245,000	$100,761	174
Public Relations Officer	14,000	119,000	37,085	125
Volunteer Coordinator	7,775	77,618	25,768	61
Chief Curator	19,300	155,000	57,256	117
Curator	10,000	124,800	50,330	121
Curator of Exhibitions	18,000	90,000	42,020	58
Associate Curator	18,170	63,000	37,739	65
Assistant Curator	11,440	53,738	30,800	53
Curatorial Assistant	9,600	55,263	22,755	83
Educator	13,000	119,000	39,893	148
Associate Educator	10,400	61,845	32,076	107
Assistant Educator	12,000	56,000	26,338	87
Educational Assistant	7,488	46,812	20,650	85
Head of Publications	17,417	99,400	44,174	64
Librarian	9,225	86,227	37,496	85

Curators—Starting salary for a curator with a Ph.D. is about $30,000 a year. A top curator will earn around $56,000 or $57,000.

Collections managers—A senior collections manager can make more than a beginning curator. Salaries range from $17,000 or $18,000 to the low $30s.

Conservators—This profession is on a similar salary scale to that of curators.

Artisans—This group falls into the same range used for educators—upper teens for entry level to the 40s for top posts.

Administration—A museum director can be paid anywhere from $70,000 to $150,000 per year.

Science Museum Salaries

The ASTC (Association of Science Technology Centers) periodically (perhaps two or three times a decade) conducts a salary survey, soliciting information from museums with a range of annual operating budgets. In addition, occasionally museums will conduct their own survey to compare their institution against others in the field. In 1995 one such salary survey was conducted by David Penn, Director of Human Resources at the Orlando Science Center. Excerpts from his survey as well as the ASTC survey are highlighted here for a variety of professional positions.

Position	Lowest Salary	Highest Salary	Mean Salary
Salaries in Science Museums			
Executive Director	$32,926	$90,618	$59,011
Director of Education	21,000	38,613	28,391
Director of Marketing	19,872	43,576	33,287
Director of Exhibits	20,644	38,213	28,552
Graphic Arts Manager	21,525	26,918	23,891
Exhibit Design Manager	20,644	29,321	23,207
Volunteer Coordinator	7,775	25,029	18,902

Salaries in Planetariums

Salaries range from institution to institution, but even in the bigger, high-cost cities, salaries are far from glamourous. A producer with experience could expect to earn from $30,000 to $40,000. Artists and photographers earn in the twenties, technicians in the low to high twenties, an astronomer and educational coordinator in the high twenties to low thirties, and the administrative positions, such as director, earn in the thirties to forties.

Salaries for Character Interpreters, Presenters, and Tour Guides

Often these are volunteer positions, but when a museum can afford to pay a professional staff, character interpreters, presenters, and tour guides can expect to earn an hourly wage, anywhere from $7.50 to $10.00 an hour.

RELATED FIELDS

The skills used by the careers discussed in this chapter are also important to the teaching profession in general, at all levels and in all settings. Other related careers include librarians, archivists, writers, journalists, and broadcasters, all highlighted in other chapters throughout this book.

INTERVIEW

Noreen Grice
Education Coordinator/Astronomer,
Charles Hayden Planetarium,
Museum of Science Boston

Noreen Grice earned a bachelor's in astronomy from Boston University in 1985 and her master's in astronomy from San Diego State University in 1987.

What the Job's Really Like

"My position is not really a research position. It's more of an educator and liaison between research and the general public. It's a mixed bag. Because I'm the person on staff with an astronomy background, I'm involved in translating the research into information we can present to the public and checking the scientific accuracy of our scripts. I'm also one of the presenters for the shows.

"I'm involved more in the early stages of the production. We have an outside writer for scripts who takes my information to write the script. It is then presented to the producer, who will then distribute it to the rest of the staff to read for how the story flows. But what I look more for is its accuracy, and it usually goes back and forth with the writer.

"I also coordinate special events such as Astronomy Day and Space Week. Astronomy Day is an international event, a day to get some extra interest in astronomy going. I'll contact all the astronomy clubs and the little planetariums in the area and ask them to come and set up a display table and we'll fill the corridors of the museum with astronomy. We have special shows and at night we'll have a star party and I'll arrange to have different speakers come in and talk on different topics.

"Space Week is always celebrated July 16 to July 24. That's more of an aerospace type of focus, NASA and rockets and moon missions.

"I also teach courses. When I came here, the only courses the planetarium offered was a naked-eye astronomy class, a telescopic astronomy class, and two navigation courses, and these were all for adults. The classes were too specialized, they catered only to adults who were interested in boating or buying a telescope. We didn't have any kids' courses and there were always parents calling up asking for one. So I created courses ranging from preschool all the way up to high school. We cover the earth and moon, sun and stars, the planets of our solar system. One is called Galaxies and Other Weird Stuff, another is Astronaut Adventure.

"I also teach a photography course for adults called Star Trails. People bring their cameras into the planetarium and we turn on the star projector and they can photograph whatever they want, constellations, the sun or moon, or eclipses. We cover the technical aspects of photography.

"I teach two or four hours a week, but the preparation is a lot more. I try to make it very hands-on, and the kids make sundials, constellation viewers, or models of black holes. They can take what they've made home with them.

"I have some administrative duties, organizing the planetarium's show schedule—we could have 3 to 8 shows in one day—keeping tabs on course supplies, that sort of thing.

"I also answer questions from the public and answer letters from school kids, especially around Science Fair Week. I noticed that everyone was asking the same questions. At first I wrote an individual reply to each person, but it was taking a lot of time so I came up with 15 brochures on different astronomy topics.

"I'm interested in astronomy and I'm interested in people and I think it's a good mix here in the planetarium. The downside is that working in a planetarium can isolate you. A lot of research is going on and I'm not in the midst of it as if I were in an academic setting."

How Noreen Grice Got Started

"When I started majoring in astronomy, I was like a lot of other students who weren't really sure what they wanted to do. I just started taking classes. I thought I would end up teaching in a university.

"But what attracted me to this field initially, is when I was little, we had 'Star Trek' and 'Lost in Space' on TV and I found it interesting. I guess I wanted to discover new life forms or learn about where Mr. Spock lived.

Expert Advice

"I think it's most important for a person to have a degree in astronomy, especially in this position. It would be very difficult to read over material for scientific accuracy without a foundation. It would give you an edge over the competition and peace of mind knowing in your heart that what you're reading is accurate. When we do a show, my name's on the dome and I don't want to put my seal of approval on anything unless I'm sure.

"Physics, earth science, and education would give you skills in teaching but not interpreting. The way planetariums are set up, you have a group of researchers out there making the discoveries. The person in the planetarium needs to know how to interpret what that research is and understand its relevance."

• • •

INTERVIEW

Carolyn Travers
Director of Research, Plimoth Plantation, Plymouth, Massachusetts

At Plimoth Plantation you can listen to seventeenth-century Goodwife Cook plan her day, or share tidbits of gossip with Governor Bradford's sister-in-law. John Alden is there, making barrels in his one-room cottage, or helping other villagers erect a new house. Not too far away, seventeenth-century sailors swab the decks or repair the lines on the Mayflower II, while passengers discuss their worries surviving the first winter in the New World.

Without the efforts of people such as Carolyn Travers, the ability to recreate authentic period characters, to accurately restore historic buildings, or to reproduce a facsimile of daily life would be an impossible task.

What the Job's Really Like

"We have four sites at Plimoth Plantation: the 1627 Pilgrim Village; the *Mayflower II;* Hobbamock's Homesite, a Wampanogg Indian site; and the Carriage House Crafts Center. We research anything we need for our program, from what is the period attitude toward toads, how a character felt about being her husband's third wife, the correct way to cook a particular dish, to some obscure point of Calvinist theology. The women are more difficult to research than the men because there is less documented information on them. You're forced into recreating a more typical persona than the actual character, sort of a generic portrayal. In general, we research the life and genealogical background and social history for all the characters we portray.

"In our research we use a variety of sources—court records and genealogical research done by professional genealogists such as the General Society of Mayflower Descendants, or writers for the *American Genealogist* or other genealogy periodicals.

"We also have researchers in other departments. For example, the authenticity of buildings and structures is done more by our curatorial department."

How Carolyn Travers Got Started

"I attended Earlham College, a small Quaker school in Richmond, Indiana, where I earned a B.A. in Fine Arts with a concentration in history. I then went on to Simmons Graduate School of Library and Information Science in Boston and graduated in 1981 with an M.S. in L.I.S. (Master's in Library and Information Science) with a concentration in research methods.

"I grew up in Plymouth and started work at the age of 14 as a part-time Pilgrim. After I finished my master's degree I returned to Plimoth Plantation as a researcher."

Expert Advice

"Researching is a competitive field, and a higher degree, in history or library science with a research methods concentration, is necessary.

"You wouldn't be expected to have a general body of knowledge about the specific time period, but you must have strong research skills, talent, and experience.

"And, as a new graduate you might begin only with a salary as low as the mid-teens. But, you don't do it for the money. There are a lot of psychological payments. One of the satisfactions is to be able to change someone's mind about the stereotypes surrounding early colonists."

• • •

INTERVIEW
Jeremy Fried
Character Interpreter, Colonial Williamsburg

The most visible living history museum employees are the scores of men and women decked out in authentic period costumes. They can be found waiting inside the buildings or walking through the grounds, and although they might seem to be there just for decoration—or "photo opportunities" as they are sometimes called—most are trained researchers, actors, and presenters. A select group of these staff members use "first-person" interpretation or role-playing to explain about their place in history. They are called "Character Interpreters" or "People of the Past." They are in actuality skilled social historians who have researched early residents and have assumed their roles.

Jeremy Fried, in addition to his position as Head of Character Interpreters at Williamsburg, has been interpreting the role of James Hubard, a colonial lawyer, off and on for the last ten years.

What the Job's Really Like

"My character spends most of his time in chambers, a fair-sized room in the courthouse, with a table in the middle seating 12 people. I sit down with a law book and quill and paper, and people come in and chat. But I don't work from a prepared script—that's what makes this form of interpretation different from other forms of living history.

"A character interpreter, often with the help of our various research departments, examines the life of an eighteenth-century person by reading available documentation—personal letters, letters to the editor, and newspapers. From this we can make inferences about their lives and what their beliefs were. As accurately as possible, we portray their ideas, their social knowledge and political opinions.

"Visitors ask questions about how I became a lawyer, about my family, about life in general in the eighteenth-century. I've had people stay with me for 1 1/2 to 2 hours. This gets to be a bit of a challenge to stay in character. But I enjoy it.

"Most full-time employees put in an 8-hour day. At least 4 of those hours are spent in the characters' natural environment—in chambers, in class at the college, in their shops or homes. The rest of the time is spent moving around town, chatting with visitors, becoming a 'photo opportunity.'

"Ample time during the week is also allocated for research or to produce facsimile newspapers in the winter months.

"Opportunities occasionally come up to move into more administrative roles. A national association of interpreters has been newly formed to let people know that interpreting history is a highly specialized skill. Right now, though, the only way to advance is to get out of interpreting and into management."

How Jeremy Fried Got Started

"I have a degree in theater from the American Academy of Dramatic Arts in New York. I'm from this area and when I graduated I moved back home and applied at Colonial Williamsburg as a character interpreter. That was more than ten years ago. I'm now involved less in character interpretation and more in administration, but I love all aspects of working at the Foundation."

Expert Advice

"The most important qualifications an applicant should possess are the ability to communicate with people, a pleasing personality, and an inquisitive mind. Of course, the Foundation prefers people with a history major, but the flip side is, unless you've done your master's thesis on colonial Virginian society, you're still going to have to do the research. You could have only a GED but still be able to formulate ideas and coordinate information.

"We have a number of folks with history degrees, but we also have a retired florist and a former petty officer in the navy. It's a mixed bag of backgrounds.

"In addition, candidates would have to be age and sex appropriate for a particular character they might be asked to play.

"And an applicant would have to be willing to accept a pretty low pay range. But, offsetting the low salaries is that the people really enjoy working for the Foundation. It's a nice work environment. The biggest stress is being hospitable to folks on vacation. And that's not a bad situation."

● ● ●

INTERVIEW

Charles McGovern
Curator, National Museum of American History
Smithsonian Institution

Curators are specialists in a particular academic discipline relevant to a museum's collections. They are generally responsible for the care and interpretation of all objects and specimens on loan or belonging to the museum, and they are fully knowledgeable about each object's history and importance.

Depending upon the museum and their area of interest, curators can work with textiles and costumes, paintings, memorabilia, historic structures, crafts, furniture, coins, or a variety of other historically significant items.

Charles McGovern is supervisor of the American History Museum's division of Community Life, overseeing a group of technicians, specialists, collections-based researchers, curators, and support staff. He is also a curator, responsible for Twentieth Century Consumerism and Popular Culture. This department covers the history of entertainment, leisure, recreation, and commerce.

The exhibits within this department are probably the most popular and the most well-known. Visitors to the museum come to view Judy Garland's ruby slippers from <u>The Wizard of Oz</u>, Archie Bunker's well-worn chair, or Edgar Bergen's famous wooden dummy, Charlie McCarthy.

What the Job's Really Like

"Part of my profession as an historian is to be a decoder or an explainer, to go back into the heads and the lives and the beliefs of our ancestors. And here, we try to do that respectfully, understanding the world as they saw it. As we do that, we see how culture reflects the times, the fears and ideals and problems of a given society. You cannot look at certain creations of our popular culture without seeing those kinds of elements in them.

"As a curator I am responsible for the creation and maintenance of the collections in my subject area. I document the history of the everyday life of American people. The major outline for my job puts me in charge of building collections, developing exhibitions, conducting research, writing, public service, public speaking, and being a graduate advisor to 11 research fellows.

"Specifically, my job is divided into three parts: acquisitions—acquiring new objects and exhibits for the museum; exhibiting and interpreting; and research.

"The collections I am responsible for include a lot of the things related to the history of American entertainment: a hat that Jimmy Durante used in his stage appearances; Ann Miller's tap shoes; Howdy Doody; Mr. Moose and Bunny Rabbit and the Grandfather clock from 'Captain Kangaroo'; the suit of armor worn by Francis X. Bushman in the original 1936 movie, *Ben Hur*; Carol Burnett's char lady costume; Mister Rogers' sweater; Harrison Ford's Indiana Jones outfit, his leather jacket and hat; Tom Selleck's ring from 'Magnum, P.I.' and his Hawaiian shirt and baseball cap; old 78 rpm records; movie posters; and comic books. We also look for collections that give us insight into American consumerism and commerce. We have the bonnet that was worn by the woman who posed for the Sunmaid raisin box, a huge collection of turn-of-the-century advertising, marketing and packaging items from the Hills Brothers Coffee Company, and a collection of memorabilia from World Fairs from 1851 to 1988.

"To build our collections we depend largely on people donating items. In fact, almost everything has been donated. We have very little money in our acquisitions budget. We can't compete in a very inflated market with the galleries and people who deal with 'collectibles.' People must be willing to donate, so we look for people who either don't need the money or who get the point of what we're trying to do.

"Sometimes we're not able to accept everything that is being offered. Someone called once and wanted to donate Charlie Chaplin's cane. But first, how do I know that it was his cane? It's impossible to document that. And second, Chaplin probably went through thousands of canes. Those bamboo things snapped very easily. Something like that we couldn't take.

"And although I must be familiar with every piece's history, the range and variety of items I am responsible for is staggering. It's not as if I were a curator of paintings where I'm trained in oils and brush techniques. Once in a while I have to confer with an appraiser or dealer to determine authenticity.

"Once a donation has been accepted, we can never promise that it will go on display. Less than 2 percent of our collection is on display at any given time, the rest is kept in storage. Although some exhibits, such as the ruby slippers or Archie's chair, are permanent, others rotate.

"Part of my job is to decide what gets exhibited, what gets stored, what is rotated. And to care for all the items, to make sure they don't deteriorate, we need to remove even permanent exhibits from time to time. People travel a long way expecting to see a certain item, and if it's not on display they're usually upset. They don't realize they should check with us first if they're coming to see something in particular. We took Charlie McCarthy off to clean him one day, and within a half an hour we had three phone calls saying where was Charlie McCarthy.

"The exhibiting side of my job is really a team effort. Exhibit designers work with curators to decide *how* an item should be displayed. The designer is responsible for the layout of objects and text and graphics and props. A conservator, someone who takes care of the actual repair or maintenance of an object, would be responsible for the 'prescription'—`this piece needs to be lit with no more than thirty footcandles,' for example.

"But I feel that research is really my first duty. All the collecting and exhibiting doesn't mean anything unless you have something to say. You have to figure out first what point you're making. Our point is the showing of everyday life of the American people, and for earlier times, that's something that has to be researched. Of course you do research to support the things you already have in your collection, but the research also helps you to determine what you should be out there collecting."

How Charles McGovern Got Started

"My interest in cultural history began at an early age. I watched a lot of television and listened to the radio and participated in the mass popular culture in the 1960s. My father and mother told me about the times when they were growing up, sharing stories with me about the early days of radio. When I got to high school and read books my teachers recommended, I realized that Babe Ruth and Laurel and Hardy and the Marx brothers, personalities I cared very deeply about, were as much a part of history as Calvin Coolidge or the first World War.

"I studied at Swarthmore College in Pennsylvania and finished in 1980 with a B.A. with honors in history. I immediately began graduate school at Harvard and earned my Master's of Arts (A.M.) in history in 1983 and my Ph.D. in American civilization in 1993.

"During that time, I taught history at Harvard, and then from 1986 through 1987, I was at the Smithsonian as a research fellow. In 1988 I returned to the Smithsonian as a full-time curator."

Expert Advice

"Every year the Smithsonian awards dozens of research fellowships, providing funding to Ph.D. candidates and access to museum collections.

"To be hired as a curator, candidates must have their Ph.D. or be almost finished with it. Entry-level positions include technicians and specialists and research-related jobs. Paid internships and volunteer positions are usually available and a good way to get a foot in the door.

"Jobs at the Smithsonian seldom become available, though. But because the Smithsonian has a certain reputation and skill in training, it's a good place to gain a foundation and then go out to other areas or institutions for work. An internship at the Smithsonian will go a long way in securing employment elsewhere. Sometimes really interesting work gets done in smaller museums with a more fixed mission."

• • •

INTERVIEW

Joyce Williams
Director of Special Products, Museum of Discovery and Science, Fort Lauderdale, Florida

Joyce Williams earned her B.S. in science education with a minor in adolescent psychology in 1979 from Cornell University in Ithaca, New York. She recently received her Master of Science degree in adult education/human resource development (AEHRD) at Florida International University in Miami.

What the Job's Really Like

"As Director of Special Projects, I'm mainly concerned with audience development, making sure we're reaching underrepresented populations, whether it be preschool or adolescents, or senior citizens, or people in diverse ethnic groups.

"My duties involve setting up collaborations with people in the community. When we work on a program or exhibit I will find partners in industry or other educational institutions. I have a meeting this week with the Broward Center for the Performing Arts so we can do a performing arts collaborative.

"I've been in the community for a number of years and have a lot of contacts. I think this is the route it will be going in the next century. You can't do things in isolation anymore because of the vast amount of knowledge and the limited amount of resources that each institution has. So, rather than everybody doing their own thing, and possibly working on the same thing, you try to find people who have like missions.

"They might want to reach the same audience or use the same methodology and you can work together. As an example, Motorola has a big industry, but maybe they don't have access to the general public. We might be doing a technology project. So, we could go to them for their expertise because we could never afford the state-of-the art technology that comes out every month. They might supply the technology and the content expertise, and we are the experts at displaying things and we know what the general public is looking for.

"Another example is that the library and Head Start both want to do something with us. So I'll ask what they're working on and look to see if there is any place it intersects for all three institutions. Then we can all work on that aspect. Each of us can bring something to the table and we can work together toward a common goal. We can't do everything, so our main goal is to focus on what we're good at.

"In addition to my field work, I also work with other departments, exhibits and marketing, for example. There are a lot of meetings, and counseling staff and the usual administrative duties.

"What excites me about hands-on museums is that I think they can make a difference in the lives of children and adults in showing a real application of science. Science is fascinating, but most people don't have that impression. I think that museums have a unique opportunity to bring science to life and to show that it's not something to be afraid of and that it's fun. It's also very creative and we can do it in an entertaining way. We can also make a difference in the classroom, training teachers how to use a different approach to teaching science.

"We hope that people will be more comfortable with science and perhaps even go into science as a career. It's a friendly field. And I like that we perform an important function, involving people in science. You want to do something that's going to have an impact."

How Joyce Williams Got Started

"I grew up in Cleveland where there are a lot of museums and my family took us all the time. I knew they existed, but I never saw any people there. All I saw were guards, so even though I enjoyed going to museums, I never thought of it as a possible career. And when I was in college I was not at all thinking about museum work.

"I moved to Florida and worked as a middle school and high school science teacher. One summer the director of education at the (then) Discovery Center asked me if I would like a job, just for the summer. That was in late June of 1986. By mid-summer, the director mentioned getting me a full-time position. I was interviewed the first week of August and by mid-August they had created a full-time position for me as Science Education Specialist.

"Two years later I was promoted to Associate Director of Education, and in 1993 I was offered the Director of Programs and Special Projects position. We're in a transition now, because the department has grown so much, we need to divide. So now there's a Director of Programs and my job, Director of Special Projects."

Expert Advice

"Visit museums and volunteer to see if it's what you like. What the visitor sees is not the whole picture. Find out the mission of that institution and align yourself with those missions and goals.

"To get into a museum's education department, it's a good idea to have teaching experience. Many of my colleagues have come from the classroom.

"I don't think people go to museums to be educated, they go to be entertained. A person who wants to go into this field can't be an authoritarian teacher. And they would need either a broad-based science background or a specialization in an area of science. And the arts are important, a theater background would help, as well as teaching skills and a love for people.

"You should have the substance, the entertaining delivery that makes it palatable, and the educational background to know what different ages are capable of learning and how people learn."

● ● ●

FOR MORE INFORMATION

Finding Employment

Although many museum lovers can find employment in their own hometown—in a local historic house museum or art gallery, for example—in order to broaden your opportunities, chances are you'll have to relocate. If you have a spot in mind where you'd like to work, a phone call or an introductory letter sent with your resume is a good way to start. If you would like some more ideas on possible locations, there are several directories listed in the coming chapters and in the appendices that can lead you to interesting destinations.

Because many sites are state or federally operated, you might have to obtain a special application through the state capital or from Washington, DC. Some private employers, however, such as the Colonial Williamsburg Foundation, expect job hopefuls to apply in person. They regularly post openings and operate a job hotline with recorded messages.

Many professional associations produce monthly or quarterly newsletters with job listings and upcoming internships and fellowships. Addresses of some key organizations are provided later in this chapter.

The *Official Museum Directory*, put out by the American Association of Museums, is a valuable resource found in the reference section of most libraries. In addition to its pages and pages of history museums, historic houses, buildings, and sites, it lists scores of historical and preservation societies, boards, agencies, councils, commissions, foundations, and research industries. You could decide on a region where you'd like to work, then approach your choices with a phone call, resume, and cover letter or personal visit.

The American Association of Museums (AAM) also puts out a monthly newsletter called *Aviso*. At least half of each issue is devoted to listings for employment opportunities and internships.

Finding a Job in a Science Center

The Association of Science-Technology Centers maintains a Job Bank, which each month lists job openings available at science centers throughout the United States. To find out about the Job Bank and to also receive a listing of hands-on science centers near you, contact:

ASTC
1025 Vermont Avenue NW, Suite 500
Washington, DC 20005

Job Information Service for Planetariums

The International Planetarium Society operates a job information service. To receive notification of new positions opening in the planetarium field, send up to six self-addressed stamped, envelopes to:

Director
Strasenburgh Planetarium
P.O. Box 1480
Rochester, NY 14603

Finding a Museum Studies Program

The American Association of Museums (AAM) puts out a publication called the *Guide to Museum Studies & Training in the United States*. It lists over 80 museum studies programs offering undergraduate or graduate courses or both. Most of these programs came into existence after 1975, and many new programs continue to join the ranks each year.

Some of the undergraduate programs offer only a single overview course supplemented by practica or internships. Many of the graduate programs require the successful completion of six or more courses in addition to the internship.

The guide presents information about a variety of training programs and lists them by state as well as by discipline. Information about pursuing careers in the following areas is also included:

Archival management

Arts management—degree programs

Arts management—non-degree programs

Conservation training—graduate programs

Conservation training—non-degree programs

Historic preservation programs

Internship or fellowship without a degree

Internship or fellowship as part of a degree program

Mid-career training opportunities

Museum studies—bachelor's degree

Museum studies—certificate

Museum studies—graduate programs

Nonprofit management programs

Programs focusing on philanthropy, volunteerism, and not-for-profit activity

Guide to Museum Studies & Training in the United States can be purchased through the AAM bookstore. Contact:

American Association of Museums
P.O. Box 4002
Washington, DC 20042-4002

The following professional associations can be contacted for more information on careers in museums:

African-American Museum Association
P.O. Box 548
Wilberforce, OH 45384

American Anthropological Association
1703 New Hampshire Avenue NW
Washington, DC 20009

American Architectural Preservation Group, Inc.
631 Cross Avenue
Los Angeles, CA 90065-4013

American Arts Alliance
1319 F Street NW, Suite 500
Washington, DC 20004

American Association for the Advancement of Science
1333 H Street NW
Washington, DC 20005

American Association for Museum Volunteers
6307 Hardy Drive
McLean, VA 22101

American Association for State and Local History
530 Church Street, Suite 600
Nashville, TN 37219

American Association of Museums
1225 I Street NW, Suite 200
Washington, DC 20005

American Historical Association
400 A Street SE
Washington, DC 20003

American Institute for Conservation of Historic and Artistic
  Works
1717 K Street NW, Suite 301
Washington, DC 20006

American Institute of Architects
1735 New York Avenue, NW
Washington, DC 20006

Archaeological Conservancy
415 Orchard Drive
Santa Fe, NM 87501

Archaeological Institute of America
675 Commonwealth Avenue
Boston, MA 02215

Archives of American Art
Administrative Office
Smithsonian Institution
8th & G Streets NW
Washington, DC 20560

Art Dealers Association of America, Inc.
575 Madison Avenue
New York, NY 10022

Association for Living Historical Farms and Agricultural
    Museums
National Museum of American History
Room 5035
Smithsonian Institution
Washington, DC 20560

Association for Preservation Technology, International
P.O. Box 8178
Fredericksburg, VA 22404

Association for Volunteer Administration
P.O. Box 4584
Boulder, CO 80306

Association of Art Museum Directors
41 East 65th Street
New York, NY 10021

Association of College and University Museums and
    Galleries
c/o University Museum
Southern Illinois University at Edwardsville
Edwardsville, IL 62026-1150

Association of Railway Museums
4131 Franklin Street, Suite 11
San Francisco, CA 94123

Association of Science Museum Directors
c/o National Museum of Natural History
Smithsonian Institution
Washington, DC 20560

Association of Science Technology Centers
1025 Vermont Avenue NW, Suite 500
Washington, DC 20005

Association of Systematics Collections
(Natural History Museums)
730 11th Street NW, 2nd Floor
Washington, DC 20001

Association of Youth Museums
c/o Children's Museum of Memphis
1515 Central Avenue
Memphis, TN 38104

Astronomical League
c/o Gary Tomlinson, Associate Curator
Roger B. Chaffee Planetarium
Grand Rapids Public Museum
233 Washington, SE
Grand Rapids, MI 49503

Council for Museum Anthropology
Southwest Museum
P.O. Box 41558
Los Angeles, CA 90041-0558

Council of American Jewish Museums
c/o The Judaica Museums at the Hebrew Home for the
    Aged at Riverdale
5961 Palisade Avenue
Bronx, NY 10471

Council of American Maritime Museums
c/o South Street Seaport Museum
207 Front Street
New York, NY 10038

Independent Curators Incorporated
799 Broadway, Suite 205
New York, NY 10003

Internship Program, Office of Museum Programs
Smithsonian Institution
Arts & Industries Building, Room 2235
Washington, DC 20560

International Association of Museum Facility
    Administrators
P.O. Box 1505
Washington, DC 20013-1505

International Council of Monuments and Sites
U.S. Committee (US/ICOMOS)
Decatur House
1600 H Street, NW
Washington, DC 20006

International Institute for Conservation-Canadian
    Group (IIC-CG)
P.O. Box 9195
Ottawa, Ontario K1G 3T9
Canada

International Museum Theatre Alliance
Museum of Science
Science Park
Boston, MA 02114-1099

International Planetarium Society
c/o Hansen Planetarium
15 South State Street
Salt Lake City, UT 84111

Medical Museum Association
Museum of Medical History
1100 Euclid Avenue
Cleveland, OH 44106-1714

Museum Computer Network
c/o Research and Scholar Office
National Museum of American Art
Smithsonian Institution
Washington, DC 20560

Museum Education Roundtable
P.O. Box 506
Beltsville, MD 20705

Museum Reference Center
Office of Museum Programs
A&I Building, Room 2235
Smithsonian Institution
Washington, DC 20560

Museum Store Association
One Cherry Center, Suite 460
Denver, CO 80222

National Center for the Study of History
Career Project
Rural Route #1, P.O. Box 679
Cornish, ME 04020

National Genealogical Society
4527 Seventeenth Street, N.
Arlington, VA 22207-2399

National Institute for the Conservation of Cultural
   Property, Inc.
3299 K Street, NW, Suite 403
Washington, DC 20007

National Register of Historic Places
U.S. Department of the Interior National Park Service
P.O. Box 37127
Washington, DC 20013-7127

National Trust for Historic Preservation
1785 Massachusetts Avenue, NW
Washington, DC 20036

Oral History Association
1093 Broxton Avenue, #720
Los Angeles, CA 90024

Organization of American Historians
112 N. Bryan Street
Bloomington, IN 47408

Popular Culture Association
Bowling Green University
Bowling Green, OH 43403

Society for American Archaeology
808 Seventeenth Street NW, Suite 200
Washington, DC 20006-3953

Society of American Historians
610 Fayerweather Hall
Columbia University
New York, NY 10027

Society of Architectural Historians
1232 Pine Street
Philadelphia, PA 19107

Society of Systematic Biologists
Museum of Natural History
NHB 163 Smithsonian
Washington, DC 20560

Space Week International Association
1110 NASA Rd. 1, Ste. 100
Houston, TX 77058

Urban History Association
History Department
Lake Forest College
555 N. Sheridan Road
Lake Forest, IL 60045

Victorian Society in America
219 S. Sixth Street
Philadelphia, PA 19106

World Monuments Fund
174 E. 80th Street
New York, NY 10021

REGIONAL MUSEUM ASSOCIATIONS

New England Museums Association
Boston National Historical Park
Charleston Navy Yard
Boston, MA 02129

Mid-Atlantic Association of Museums
P.O. Box 817
Newark, DE 19715-0817

Southeastern Museums Conference
P.O. Box 3494
Baton Rouge, LA 70821

Midwest Museums Conference
P.O. Box 11940
St. Louis, MO 63112

Mountain-Plains Museum Association
Box 335
Manitou Springs, CO 80829

Western Museums Conference
700 State Street, Room 130
Los Angeles, CA 90037

CHAPTER 8 Librarians and Archivists

OVERVIEW

Librarians

Librarians make information available to people. They manage staff, oversee the collection and cataloging of library materials, and develop and direct information programs for the public. They help users find information from printed and other materials.

Library work is divided into three basic functions:

User services

Technical services

Administrative services

Librarians in user services, for example, reference and children's librarians, work directly with users to help them find the information they need. This may involve analyzing users' needs to determine what information is appropriate, and searching for, acquiring, and providing the information to users.

Librarians in technical services, such as acquisitions librarians and catalogers, acquire and prepare materials for use and may not deal directly with the public.

Librarians in administrative services oversee the management of the library, supervising library employees, preparing budgets, and directing activities to see that all parts of the library function properly. Depending on the employer, librarians may perform a combination of user, technical, and administrative services.

In small libraries or information centers, librarians generally handle all aspects of the work. They read book reviews, publishers' announcements, and catalogs to keep up with current literature and other available resources, and select and purchase materials from publishers, wholesalers, and distributors.

Librarians prepare new materials for use by classifying them by subject matter, and describe books and other library materials in a way that users can easily find them. They supervise assistants who prepare cards, computer records, or other access tools that indicate the title, author, subject, publisher, date of publication, and location in the library.

In large libraries, librarians often specialize in a single area, such as acquisitions, cataloging, bibliography, reference, special collections, circulation, or administration.

Librarians also compile lists of books, periodicals, articles, and audiovisual materials on particular subjects, and recommend materials to be acquired. They may collect and organize books, pamphlets, manuscripts, and other materials in a specific field, such as rare books, genealogy, or music.

In addition, they coordinate programs such as storytelling for children and book talks for adults; publicize services; provide reference help; supervise staff; prepare the budget; and oversee other administrative matters.

Librarians may be classified according to the type of library in which they work:

Public libraries

School library/media centers

Academic libraries

Special libraries

They may work with specific groups, such as children, young adults, adults, or disadvantaged individuals. In school library/media centers, librarians help teachers develop curricula, acquire materials for classroom instruction, and sometimes team teach.

Librarians may also work in information centers or libraries maintained by government agencies, corporations, law firms, advertising agencies, museums, professional associations, medical centers, religious organizations, and research laboratories.

They build and arrange the organization's information resources, usually limited to subjects of special interest to the organization. These special librarians can provide vital information services by preparing abstracts and indexes of current periodicals, organizing bibliographies, or analyzing background information on areas of particular interest. For instance, a special librarian working for a corporation may provide the sales department with information on competitors or new developments affecting their field.

Many libraries are tied into remote databases through their computer terminals, and many also maintain their own computerized databases. The widespread use of automation in libraries makes database searching skills important to librarians. Librarians develop and index databases and help users develop searching skills to obtain the information they need.

Libraries may employ automated systems librarians who plan and operate computer systems, and information scientists who design information storage and retrieval systems and develop procedures for collecting, organizing, interpreting, and classifying information.

The increasing use of automated information systems enables some librarians to spend more time analyzing future information needs as well as on administrative and budgeting responsibilities, and to delegate more technical and user services to technicians.

Working conditions in user services are different from those in technical services. Assisting users in obtaining the information for their jobs or for recreational and other needs can be challenging and satisfying. When working with users under deadlines, the work may be busy, demanding, and stressful.

In technical services, selecting and ordering new materials can be stimulating and rewarding. However, librarians may sit at desks or at computer terminals all day. Extended work at video display terminals may cause eyestrain and headaches.

They may also have their performance monitored for errors or for quantity of tasks completed each hour or day.

Nearly one out of four librarians works part time. Public and college librarians often work weekends and evenings. School librarians generally have the same workday schedule as classroom teachers and similar vacation schedules. Special librarians usually work normal business hours.

Librarians in fast-paced industries, such as advertising or legal services, may work over 40 hours a week under stressful conditions.

Archivists

Archivists handle collections that chart the course of daily life for individuals and businesses. Some archives specifically look after materials created by their own institution. Coca Cola Co., for example, set up an archives years ago to have a history of what the company business was and how it prospered. New companies set up archives to keep a documented record.

Other institutions, such as universities or museums, create archives that relate to their special research interests.

Nobody knows the exact number, but it's estimated that there are close to 5,000 archives in the United States. Each of the 50 states maintains a government archives as well as do most city and county governments. Archives will also be found in universities, historical societies, museums, libraries, and private businesses.

On the national level, there is the National Archives in Washington, DC, which looks after the records of the federal government. The Library of Congress provides information services to the U.S. Congress and technical services to all the libraries across the country.

Although archives are similar to libraries, there are distinct differences between the two. Libraries typically house materials that are published and were created with the express purpose of broad dissemination. Archives typically hold materials that were created in the course of carrying out some sort of business or activity, but were never intended originally for public dissemination. For example, in an archives you might find letters from a Civil War soldier to his family. He wrote about his experiences and feelings and to let his loved ones know that he was still alive, surviving this or that battle. He never would have imagined that his correspondence would one day appear in an archives. This gives his letters credibility, an integrity as a historical source. The newspaper reporter covering the same battles is writing with a specific point of view for broadspread publication, ultimately with the intention of selling newspapers.

The material found in an archives can be letters, personal papers, organizational records, and other documents. Archives created within the last 100 years or so could also contain visual records such as photographs and postcards, prints, drawings, and sketches.

Today, also collected and archived are recording tapes, phonograph records, movie films, videotapes, and computer-stored information.

Because archives hold firsthand information, they are valuable to anyone with an interest in the people, places, and events of the past. This group includes genealogists, museum researchers, scholars and students, writers, and historians.

TRAINING

Librarians

A master's degree in library science (M.L.S.) is necessary for librarian positions in most public, academic, and special libraries, and in some school libraries. In the federal government, an M.L.S. or the equivalent in education and experience is needed. Many colleges and universities offer M.L.S. programs, but many employers prefer graduates of the approximately 60 schools accredited by the American Library Association. Most M.L.S. programs require a bachelor's degree; any liberal arts major is appropriate.

Some programs take one year to complete; others take two. A typical graduate program includes courses in the foundations of library and information science, including the history of books and printing, intellectual freedom and censorship, and the role of libraries and information in society. Other basic courses cover material selection and processing; the organization of information; reference tools and strategies; and user services. Course options include resources for children or young adults; classification, cataloging, indexing, and abstracting; library administration; and library automation.

The M.L.S. provides general, all-round preparation for library work, but some people specialize in a particular area such as archives (see below), media, or library automation.

A Ph.D. degree in library and information science is advantageous for a college teaching or top administrative position, particularly in a college or university library or in a large library system.

In special libraries, a knowledge of the subject specialization, or a master's, doctoral, or professional degree in the subject is highly desirable. Subject specializations include medicine, law, business, engineering, and the natural and social sciences. For example, a librarian working for a law firm may also be a licensed attorney, holding both library science and law degrees. In some jobs, knowledge of a foreign language is needed.

State certification requirements for public school librarians vary widely. Most states require that school librarians—often called library media specialists—be certified as teachers and have courses in library science. In some cases, an M.L.S., perhaps with a library media specialization, or a master's in education with a specialty in school library media or educational media is needed. Some states require certification of public librarians employed in municipal, county, or regional library systems.

Experienced librarians may advance to administrative positions, such as department head, library director, or chief information officer.

Archivists

The standard way to become an archivist is to have an undergraduate degree with a history background, and a graduate degree at least at the master's level that would involve specific course work in archives. There are 30 to 50 programs (the Society of American Archivists publishes a directory of these educational programs), which are often in graduate library schools.

Many archivists have a Master of Library Science degree (M.L.S.) with a concentration in archives, but sometimes archives courses are also taught in history departments.

Archivists need analytical ability to understand the content of documents and the context in which they were created, and to decipher deteriorated or poor-quality printed matter, handwritten manuscripts, or photographs and films. Archivists also must be able to organize large amounts of information and write clear instructions for its retrieval and use.

JOB OUTLOOK

Librarians

Employment of librarians is expected to grow more slowly than the average for all occupations through the year 2005. The limited growth in employment of librarians during the 1980s is expected to continue. However, the number of job openings resulting from the need to replace librarians who leave the occupation is expected to increase by 2005, as many workers reach retirement age. Willingness to relocate will greatly enhance job prospects.

Budgetary constraints will likely contribute to the slow growth in employment of librarians in school, public, and college and university libraries. The increasing use of computerized information storage and retrieval systems may also dampen the demand for librarians. For example, computerized systems make cataloging easier, and this task can now be handled by other library staff.

In addition, many libraries are equipped for users to access library computers directly from their homes or offices. These systems allow users to bypass librarians and conduct research on their own. However, librarians will be needed to help users develop database searching techniques and to define users' needs.

Childrens' librarians will be the least affected by information technology because children need special assistance.

Opportunities will be best for librarians outside traditional settings. Nontraditional library settings include information brokers, private corporations, and consulting firms. Many companies are turning to librarians because of their excellent research and organizational skills, and knowledge of library automation systems.

Librarians can review the vast amount of information that is available and analyze, evaluate, and organize it according to acompany's specific needs. Librarians working in these settings are often classified as systems analysts, database specialists, managers, and researchers.

Archivists

Employment of archivists is expected to increase about as fast as the average for all occupations through the year 2005. Although the rate of turnover among archivists is relatively low, the need to replace workers who leave the occupation or stop working will create some additional job openings.

While federal government archival jobs are not expected to grow, new archival jobs are expected in other areas, such as educational services and state and local government. Archival jobs also will become available as institutions put more emphasis on establishing archives and organizing records and information.

Despite the anticipated increase in the employment of archivists, competition for jobs is expected to be keen. Graduates with highly specialized training, such as a master's degree in library science with a concentration in archives or records management, may have the best opportunities for jobs as archivists.

SALARIES

Librarians

Salaries of librarians vary by the individual's qualifications and the type, size, and location of the library. Based on a survey published in the *Library Journal*, starting salaries of graduates of library school master's degree programs accredited by the

American Library Association averaged $25,900 in 1992, and ranged from $23,800 in public libraries to $27,400 in school libraries. In college and university libraries, they averaged $25,400, and in special libraries, they averaged $27,700.

According to the Educational Research Service, experienced school librarians averaged about $37,900 during the 1992–93 school year.

According to the Special Libraries Association, 1992 salaries for special librarians with one to two years of library experience averaged $29,200, and those with three to five years of experience average $31,800.

Salaries for special library managers averaged $45,200.

The average annual salary for all librarians in the federal government in nonsupervisory, supervisory, and managerial positions was $44,500 in 1993.

Archivists

Archivists with a master's degree can expect to start out in the mid- to high-twenties. Someone with ten years under his or her belt working as an archivist with administrative responsibilities might earn $60,000 a year or more.

Salaries in the federal government depend upon education and experience. In 1993, inexperienced archivists with a bachelor's degree started at about $18,300, while those with some experience started at $22,700. Those with a master's degree started at $27,800, and with a doctorate, $33,600 or $40,300. In 1993, the average annual salary for archivists employed by the federal government in nonsupervisory, supervisory, and managerial positions was $46,000 a year.

RELATED FIELDS

Librarians play an important role in the transfer of knowledge and ideas by providing people with access to the information they need and want. Jobs requiring similar analytical, organizational, and communicative skills include archivists, information scientists, museum curators, publishers' representatives, research analysts, information brokers, and records managers.

The management aspect of a librarian's work is similar to the work of managers in a variety of business and government settings. School librarians have many duties similar to those of school teachers.

Archivists' interests in preservation and display are shared by anthropologists, arborists, archaeologists, artifacts conservators, botanists, ethnologists, folklorists, genealogists, historians, horticulturists, information specialists, librarians, paintings restorers, records managers, and zoologists.

INTERVIEW

Carol Jones
Technical Services and Interlibrary Loan Librarian

Carol Jones works at the Kline Science Library, one of many libraries at Yale University in New Haven, Connecticut. She has been a librarian for over 20 years.

What the Job's Really Like

"Technical services is a broad term that includes acquisitions and cataloging and binding of materials. My position is very similar to working in a business. Acquisitions means we buy materials—books and electronic resources. We have a lot of journals that are now available in an electronic format over the Internet, as opposed to being printed on paper and bound in a cover.

"The budget we have for buying materials is over a million dollars, so this is big business. Once we order those materials, we have to see that they're received and made available on the shelves. My position is administrative and I supervise four people, monitor budgets, write policies and procedures, and train people. I meet with vendors, the people from whom we buy various materials, and work on problems. I also serve on committees in the university library that have to with a wide range of issues.

"Right now a good deal of my time is also spent working with computers and the hardware and software side of things. We have a local area network and we have work stations for all of our staff and for the patrons. I do a lot of the work myself, and I also coordinate the computer work for the five other science libraries at Yale.

"I like the detail of it and the business orientation of it. I never really wanted to go into the corporate world. Academe does have nice benefits in terms of vacation time and a certain flexibility I think would be missing in a corporate setting.

"From what I've heard from friends who work in public libraries, I think I'd much prefer the university setting I'm in. The patrons are very different. The public libraries deal with current readings, they have children and adults with a real wide range of interests. We have students and faculty who are fairly focused.

"There is a considerable amount of pressure and stress with my job, though. We're not unlike many businesses right now in which there is an increasing emphasis on downsizing, resource reallocation, greater productivity with few people and that takes a toll.

"Also, the technology, which is an integral part of what we do, is changing so fast. There are times when I feel I haven't even learned one thing and it's already time to go on to the next generation after that."

How Carol Jones Got Started

"I got interested in library work when I was an undergraduate, but I was rather an old undergraduate. I was already married and had three children before I started college. My interest stemmed mainly from my own use of the library, but I didn't pursue it until my last year in college, when I started working part time in the library.

"Part of it was a love for books and an interest in publishing, information, and research. But also I did take some undergraduate classes in library science, and though many people might have found them terribly boring—cataloging of materials and organizing materials so they could be found with ease, that sort of thing—they were of great interest to me.

"Also, on a more practical level, perhaps, it offered an opportunity for a career that had a certain amount of flexibility, which was particularly important to me at that point since I did have young children.

"After that I decided to get a master's degree because I knew I wouldn't make any money unless I did that. My B.A. was in history from Kentucky Wesleyan and my master's, an M.L.S., was from the University of Kentucky in Lexington in their School of Library and Information Science.

"I worked for nine years at the library at Kentucky Wesleyan, then came to Yale in 1983 as a government documents librarian."

Expert Advice

"If anything, the field of librarianship is going to become even more interesting and more important as electronic resources are more broadly available. As information expands and expands at an ever faster rate, librarians are going to be integral in making that information understandable and accessible to the people who need some piece of it. It's one thing to say everyone will have a computer and they'll be able to do it all themselves. But in actuality, someone who is familiar with the way the information is organized and how you can get at it is going to be crucial. And that someone is going to be a librarian. Knowledge of computers and information resources is absolutely essential.

"Subject expertise and language expertise has always been useful, too, and it will be even more so in the future."

● ● ●

INTERVIEW

Steve Oserman
Reference Librarian

Steve Oserman is a reference librarian in the Adult Services Department with the Skokie Public Library in Illinois. He has more than thirty years of combined teaching and library experience. He is co-author of The Guide to Internet Job Searching with Margaret Riley and Frances Roehm and developed two books through the Job and Career Information Services Committee of the Public Library Association called The Basic Guide to Resume Writing and The Basic Guide to Cover Letter Writing. All three books are published by NTC Publishing Group.

What the Job's Really Like

"The way we have the day set up now I'm on the reference desk two hours, off two hours. At the desk I'm helping people with general reference questions on a variety of topics. I also assist people with the Internet and CD-ROMs. We have the Internet out for the public. When I'm off the desk I run the employment resource center here. I have appointments to help patrons with resumes, job changes, Internet job search strategies, whatever help they need.

"We are especially aggressive in this area, and in addition to the position I hold with the library I'm the cochair of job and career information services for the Public Library Association. So I'm doing national speaking and training to help librarians develop their expertise in helping people find jobs and start career centers.

"I also do book discussions and I do a lot of lectures and programs. I have 17 programs coming up in the next 20 days. Most all of them are on Internet job searching, but I also do lectures on dreams and health and healing for hospitals in the area. I'm also doing one for Motorola on financial resources on the Internet.

"I also trade options and do lectures on technical analysis of stock option trends. In addition, I do Chinese astrology and I-ching and I always tell people to pursue at least 7 careers simultaneously. I'm trying to have at least 14.

"I like my work a lot, but I don't like meetings and the bureaucratic paperwork. I like things that involve people. I'm very extroverted and I like helping people find jobs or motivation. And I enjoy the seminars and public speaking I do.

"I'm here officially 37 1/2 hours a week, but I spend a lot more time than that. I come in early and I come in in the evenings too. I do my committee work on my days off.

How Steve Oserman Got Started

"I have a B.S. in mathematics and philosophy from the University of Illinois at Champaign-Urbana and substantial work toward a Ph.D. in philosophy at Southern Illinois University at Carbondale, where I also taught philosophy.

"I'm atypical; I never went to library school. I started at a time when there was a shortage of librarians and got my training on the job. Plus, because I had over 200 credits of graduate work in other fields, my employers considered that as good as at least one year of library school.

"I started out with library work because it was a way to help finance my college education. It wasn't really a career I chose to go into. I was unhappy in the early years when I was doing more of the traditional librarian work, but I don't feel as stuck as I used to. Ever since I got more involved with career information areas it's been much more interesting."

Expert Advice

"This career is not just being around books; it's really being around people much more. A lot of people think they might be a good candidate for a library job just because they like to be around books, but actually, that's exactly what's not needed. There is probably a too-high percentage of introverted people who are already in the library profession, as compared to the general population. We need more extroverted people.

"There are still lots of jobs available, especially in the Midwest, compared with other jobs I've checked into, but it's not very good on the east and west coasts, where libraries are closing, and in the south. You might have to be prepared to relocate to find the best job.

"I think that it's a profession that a lot of people in it love the work they do. At seminars I've had for librarians I've been surprised at how many of them really do enjoy their work. The only problem is a lot of them would like to have more career development possibilities. A lot of librarians get plateaued where there's not enough room for advancement. This should be taken into consideration when choosing this career.

● ● ●

INTERVIEW

John Fleckner
Chief Archivist, National Museum of American History, Smithsonian Institution

John Fleckner came to the Smithsonian in 1982 with more than a decade's experience working as an archivist for the State Historical Society of Wisconsin. He is a past president of the Society of American Archivists and has acted as a consultant on many important archives projects including the United Negro College Fund, the Vietnam History and Archives Project, and the Native American Archives Project.

What the Job's Really Like

"Archivists provide a service to society by identifying and preserving materials with lasting value for the future. When archivists talk about their work, they discuss certain basic functions that are common to all archives.

"I oversee a professional staff of 12 archivists, 3 student interns, and close to 20 volunteers. About 50 percent of my time is spent in supervision. The rest covers the identification and acquisition of materials; providing reference services; handling administrative duties—meetings, budget, personnel; then there's outreach and public affairs.

"The archives I am responsible for acquires collections from the outside and does not handle the records generated by the museum. The collections cover a wide range of subjects and are particularly strong in the areas of American music, advertising, and the history of technology.

"As with libraries and archives, there are distinct differences between librarians and archivists, the way they operate, and the methods and the techniques they use to handle material.

"The biggest single difference is that librarians look at materials they get on an item-by-item basis. Each book is a distinct entity evaluated separately from the other books. In an archives, a single letter would usually be part of a larger collection of letters. Archivists are interested in these as a group, because one letter would only be a fragment. To really understand something about the past, the information needs to be synthesized and put together from a collection."

How John Fleckner Got Started

"I did my undergraduate work at Colgate, in Hamilton, N.Y., graduating in 1963 with a B.A. with honors in history. I earned my master's degree in American history at the University of Wisconsin in 1965. I have also amassed significant work toward a Ph.D.

"After too many years of graduate school, pursuing a vague notion of teaching college-level history, I realized that I really didn't want to teach. I was so naive it took a university career counselor to recognize that my history background might be anything other than an economic liability. Leaning back in her chair, she pointed out her office window to the State Historical Society of Wisconsin just across the street, and she directed me to a recently established graduate program in archives administration. The instructor would make no promises about the prospects for a job, but with a sly smile he offered that all his previous students were working. I didn't need a weatherman—as they said in those days, the early 1970s—to tell me which way the wind was blowing.

"So, it was an accident in good guidance that got me in the door. But it was the experience of doing archival work—beginning with the simplest class exercises and then a formal internship—that sealed it for me. I loved the combination of handicraft and analytical work and I loved the intense, intimate contact with the 'stuff' of history. Before I completed my internship I knew I wanted to be an archivist.

"Previously, as a graduate student, of course I had done some research in archives—at the Library of Congress, the College of William and Mary, and especially the State Historical Society. But the archivists had taken all the fun out of it—the materials were antiseptically foldered, boxed, and listed. Wheeled out on carts, they were like cadavers to be dissected by first-year medical students. On occasion I even donned white gloves. The documents always seemed lifeless.

"Later, as a would-be archivist they thrilled me. I was in charge, I would evaluate their significance, determine their order, describe their contents, and physically prepare them for their permanent resting places. Still, it was not so much this heady feeling of control that awed me but more the mystery, the possibilities of the records themselves.

"My judgments would be critical to building paths to the records for generations of researchers, across the entire spectrum of topics, and into unknown future time.

"The archival enterprise held another attractive feature for me. For all the opportunity to reconstruct the past captured in these documents, and to imagine the future research they might support, I had a well-defined task to accomplish, a product to produce, techniques and methods for proceeding, and standards against which my work would be judged. There was rigor and discipline; this was real work. And, as good fortune would have it, I soon was getting paid to do it."

Expert Advice

"People get into the archives profession in a variety of traditional and unusual ways. Often in a small town an archives is a closet in the back room of a local historical society's office. Someone volunteers to put it all together, perhaps the oldest person in the community with a strong interest in the area's history.

"But to assure a professional, paid position, I'd recommend you pursue either a degree in history with specific archives courses or a master's in library science with courses in archives administration."

• • •

FOR MORE INFORMATION

Information on librarianship, including a listing of accredited education programs and information on scholarships or loans, is available from:

American Library Association (ALA)
Office for Library Personnel Resources
50 East Huron St.
Chicago, IL 60611

For information on a career as a special librarian, write to:

Special Libraries Association
1700 18th St. NW
Washington, DC 20009

Material about a career in information science is available from:

American Society for Information Science
8720 Georgia Ave., Suite 501
Silver Spring, MD 20910

Information on graduate schools of library and information science can be obtained from:

Association for Library and Information Science Education
4101 Lake Boone Trail, Suite 201
Raleigh, NC 27607

Information on schools receiving federal financial assistance for library training is available from:

Office of Educational Research and Improvement
Library Programs
Library Development Staff
U.S. Department of Education
555 New Jersey Ave NW, Room 402
Washington, DC 20208-5571

For information on a career as a law librarian, as well as a list of ALA accredited library schools offering programs in law librarianship and scholarship information, contact:

American Association of Law Libraries
53 West Jackson Blvd., Suite 940
Chicago, IL 60604

For information on employment opportunities as a health science librarian, contact:

Medical Library Association
6 N. Michigan Ave., Suite 300
Chicago, IL 60602

Those interested in a position as a librarian in the federal service should write to:

Office of Personnel Management
1900 E St. NW.
Washington, DC 20415

Information concerning requirements and application procedures for positions in the Library of Congress may be obtained directly from:

Personnel Office
Library of Congress
101 Independence Ave. SE
Washington, DC 20540

State library agencies can furnish information on scholarships available through their offices, requirements for certification, and general information about career prospects in the state.

Several of these agencies maintain job hotlines which report openings for librarians.

State departments of education can furnish information on certification requirements and job opportunities for school librarians.

For information on archivists and on schools offering courses in archival science, contact:

Society of American Archivists
600 South Federal St., Suite 504
Chicago, IL 60605

For information about certification for archivists, contact:

Academy of Certified Archivists
600 South Federal St., Suite 504
Chicago, IL 60605

About the Author

A full-time writer of career books, Blythe Camenson's main concern is helping job seekers make educated choices. She firmly believes that with enough information, readers can find long-term, satisfying careers. To that end, she researches traditional as well as unusual occupations, talking to a variety of professionals about what their jobs are really like. In all of her books, she includes first-hand accounts from people who can reveal what to expect in each occupation, the upsides as well as the down.

Camenson's interests range from history and photography to writing novels. She is also director of Fiction Writer's Connection, a membership organization providing support to new and published writers.

Camenson was educated in Boston, earning her B.A. in English and psychology from the University of Massachusetts and her M.Ed. in counseling from Northeastern University.

In addition to *On the Job: Real People Working in Education*, the other books she has written for NTC Publishing are:

Career Portraits: Travel

Career Portraits: Writing

Career Portraits: Nursing

Career Portraits: Firefighting

Careers for History Buffs

Careers for Plant Lovers

Careers for Health Nuts

Careers for Mystery Buffs

Careers for Self-Starters

Great Jobs for Art Majors

Great Jobs for Communications Majors

Great Jobs for Liberal Arts Majors

On the Job: Real People Working in Health Care

On the Job: Real People Working in Law

On the Job: Real People Working in Sales and Marketing

Opportunities in Museums

Opportunities in Teaching English to Speakers of Other Languages